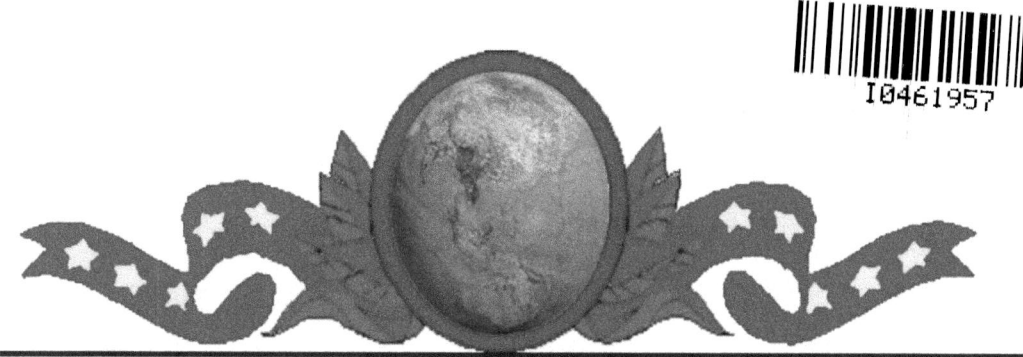

# Real World
## Colouring Book
### For Advanced Users & Adults

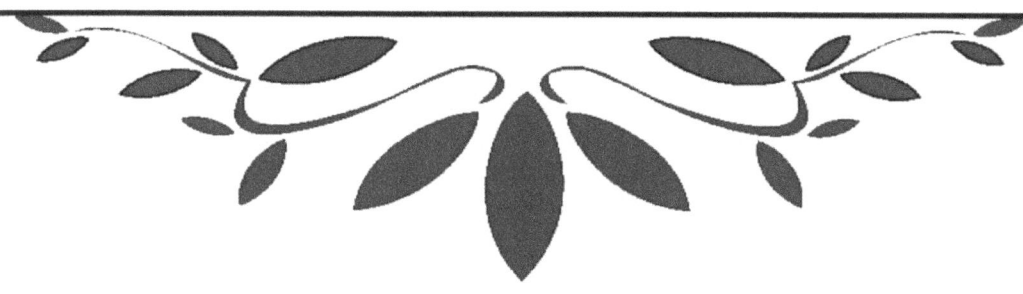

Copyright 2019 By John Boom

## 50 Images

## Created From Real Life Photos
## For You To Colour As You Please.

ISBN 978-0-359-78797-5

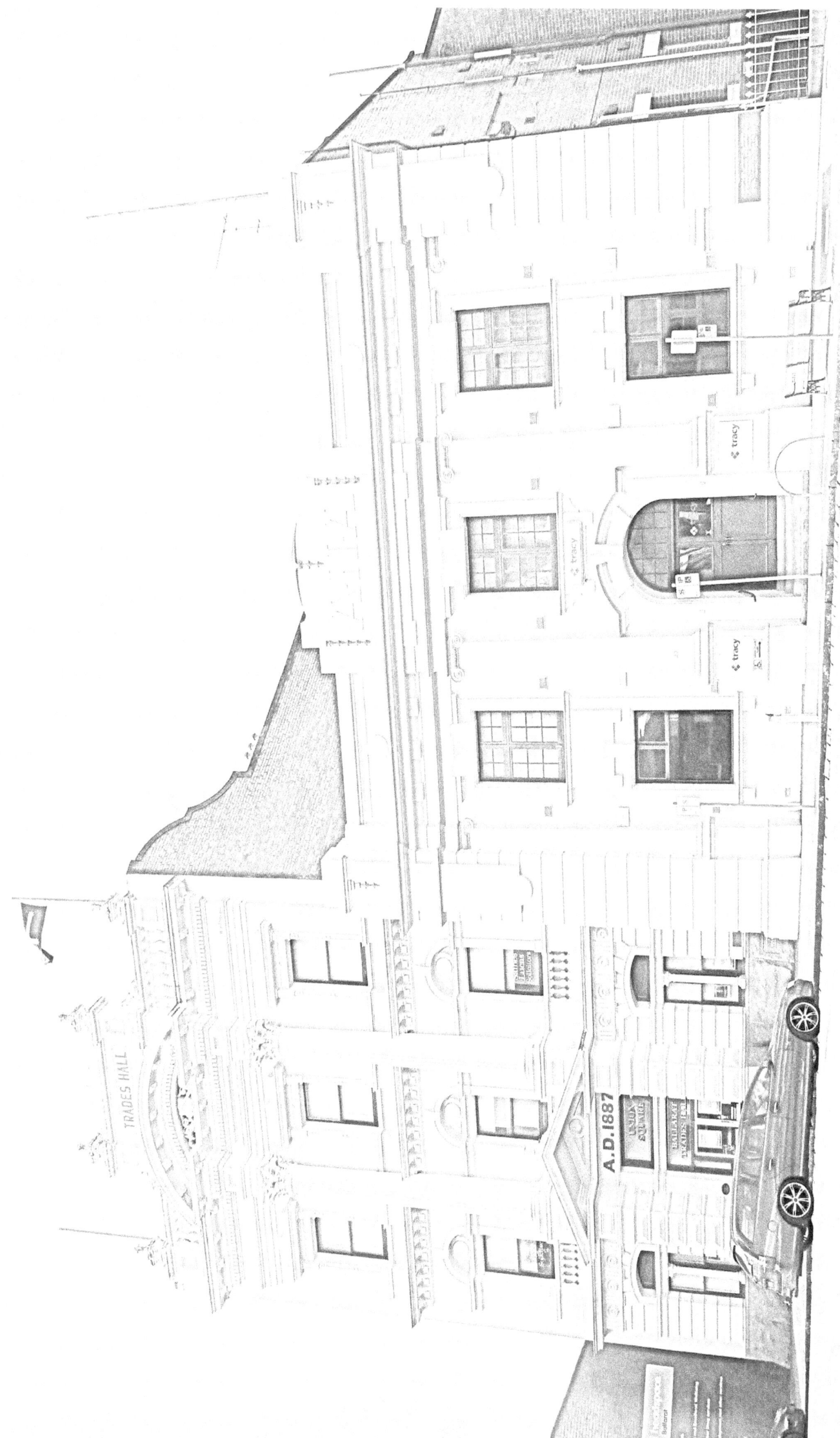

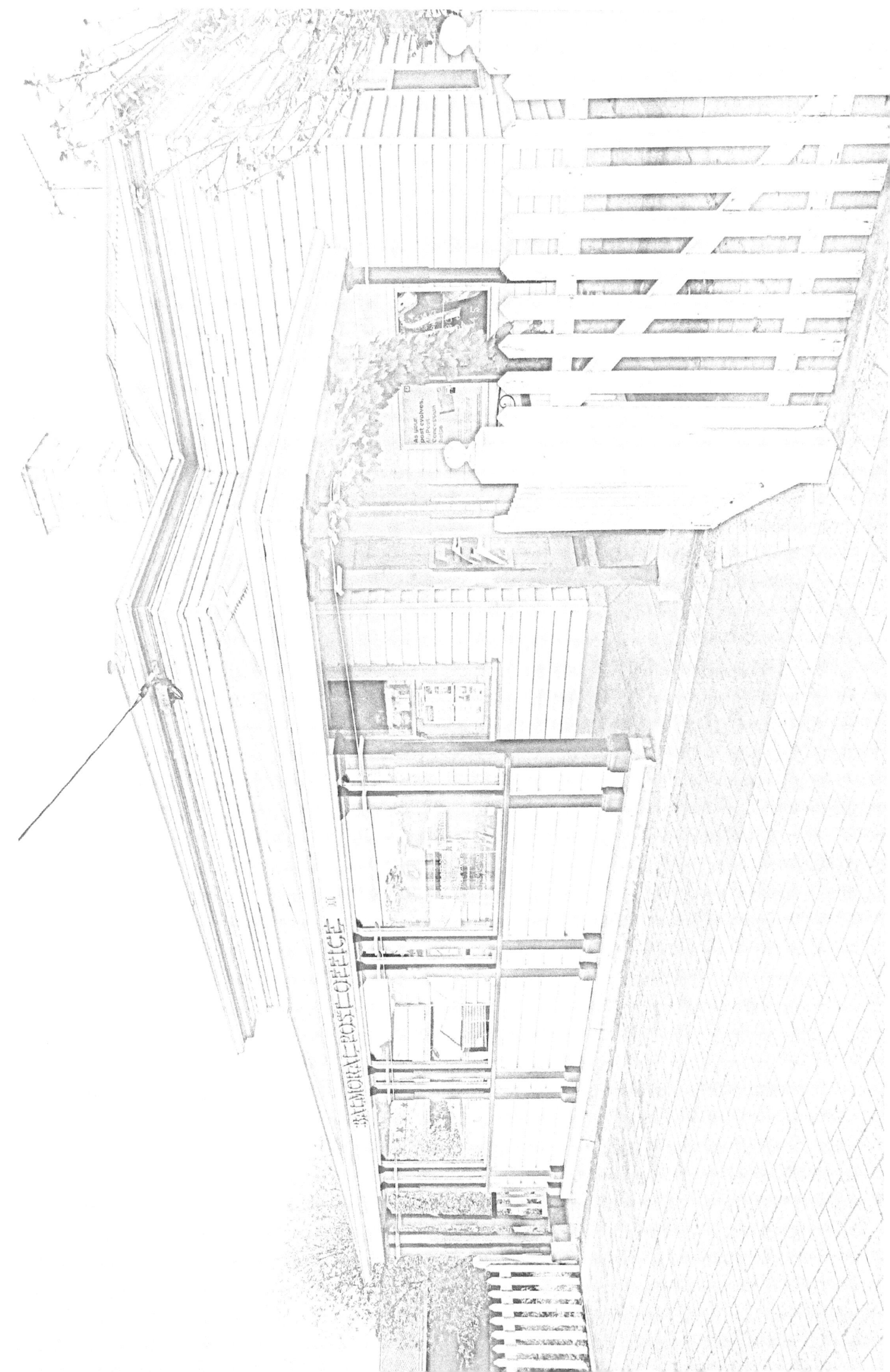

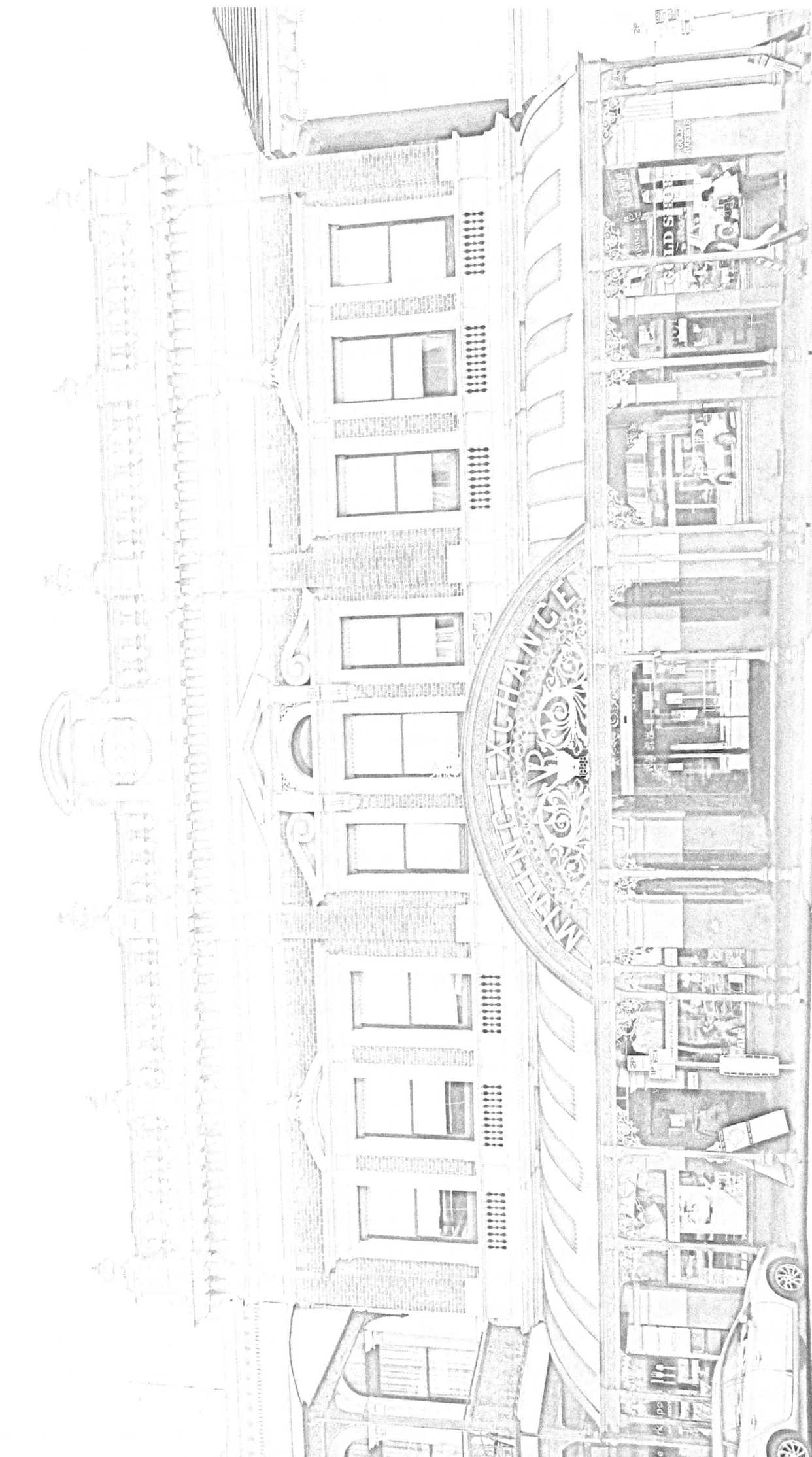

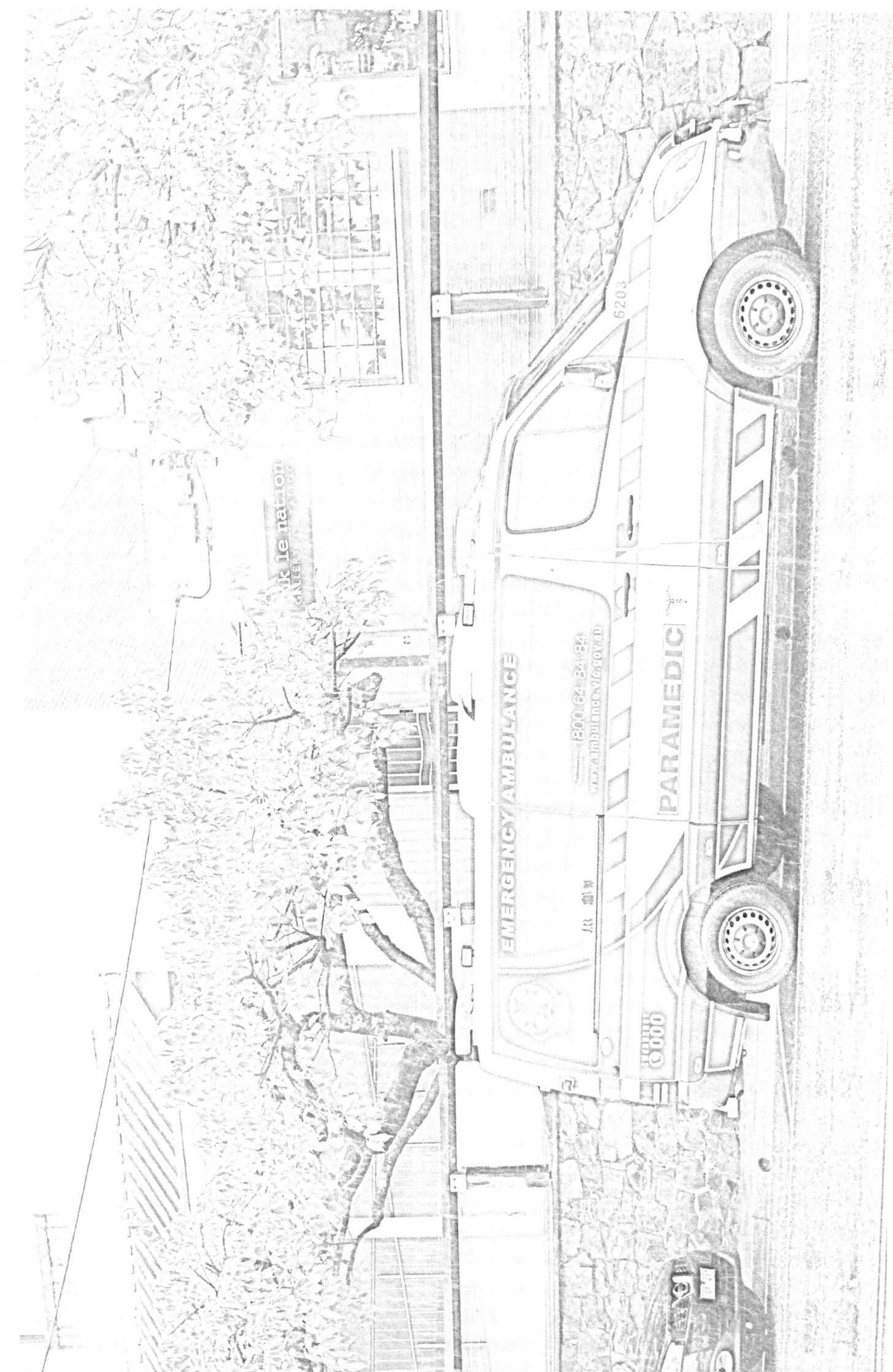

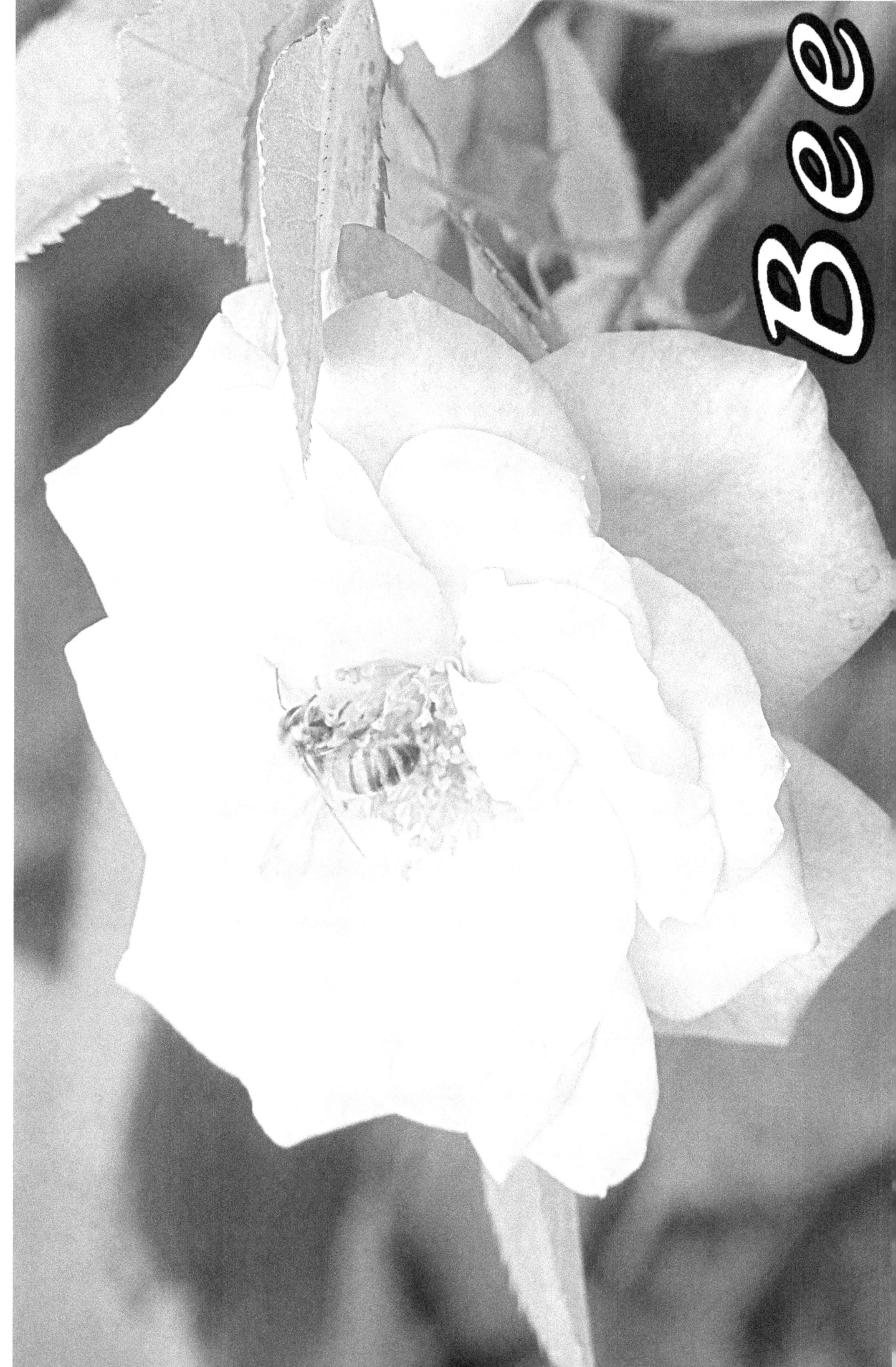

Bee

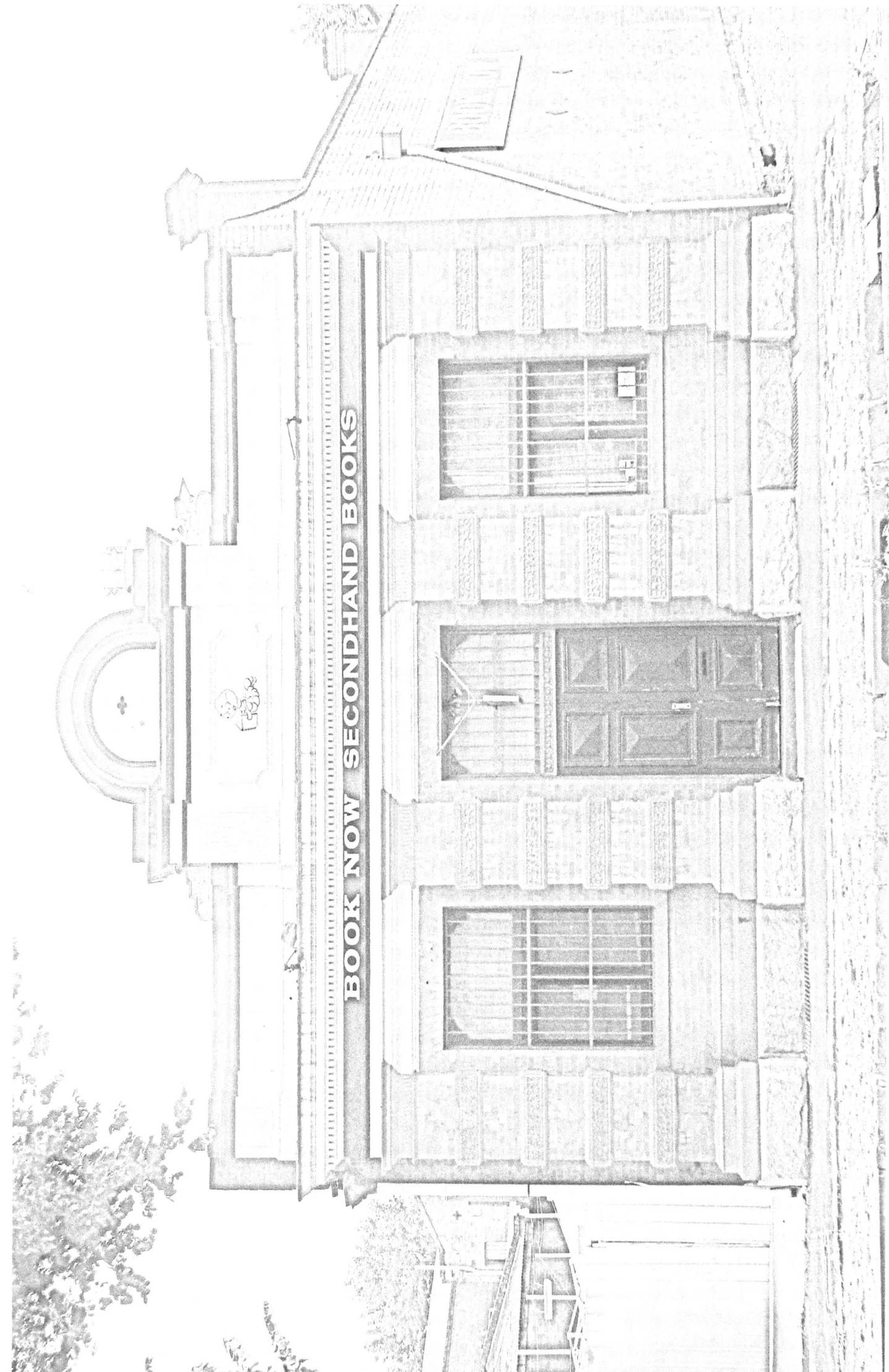

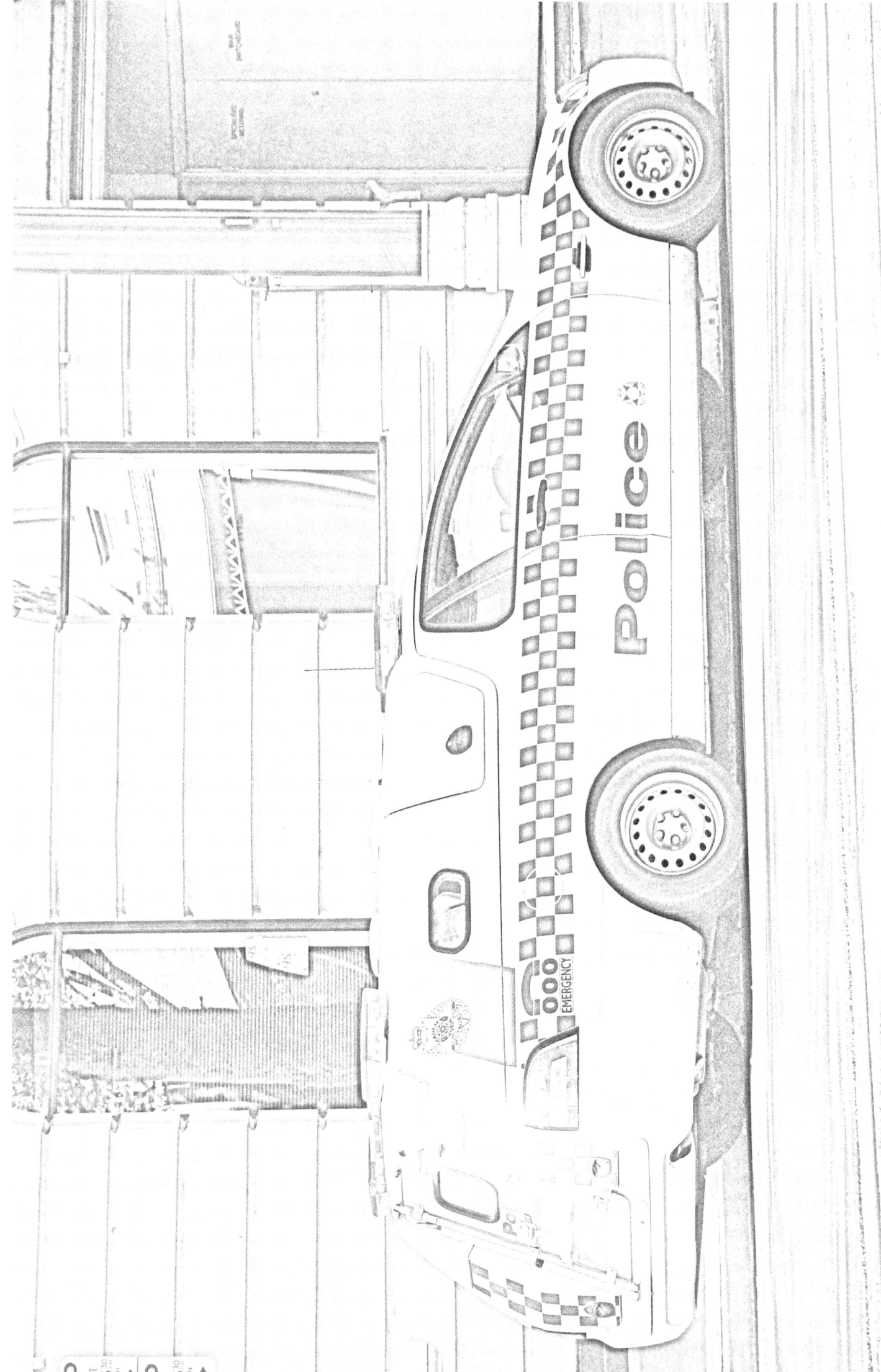

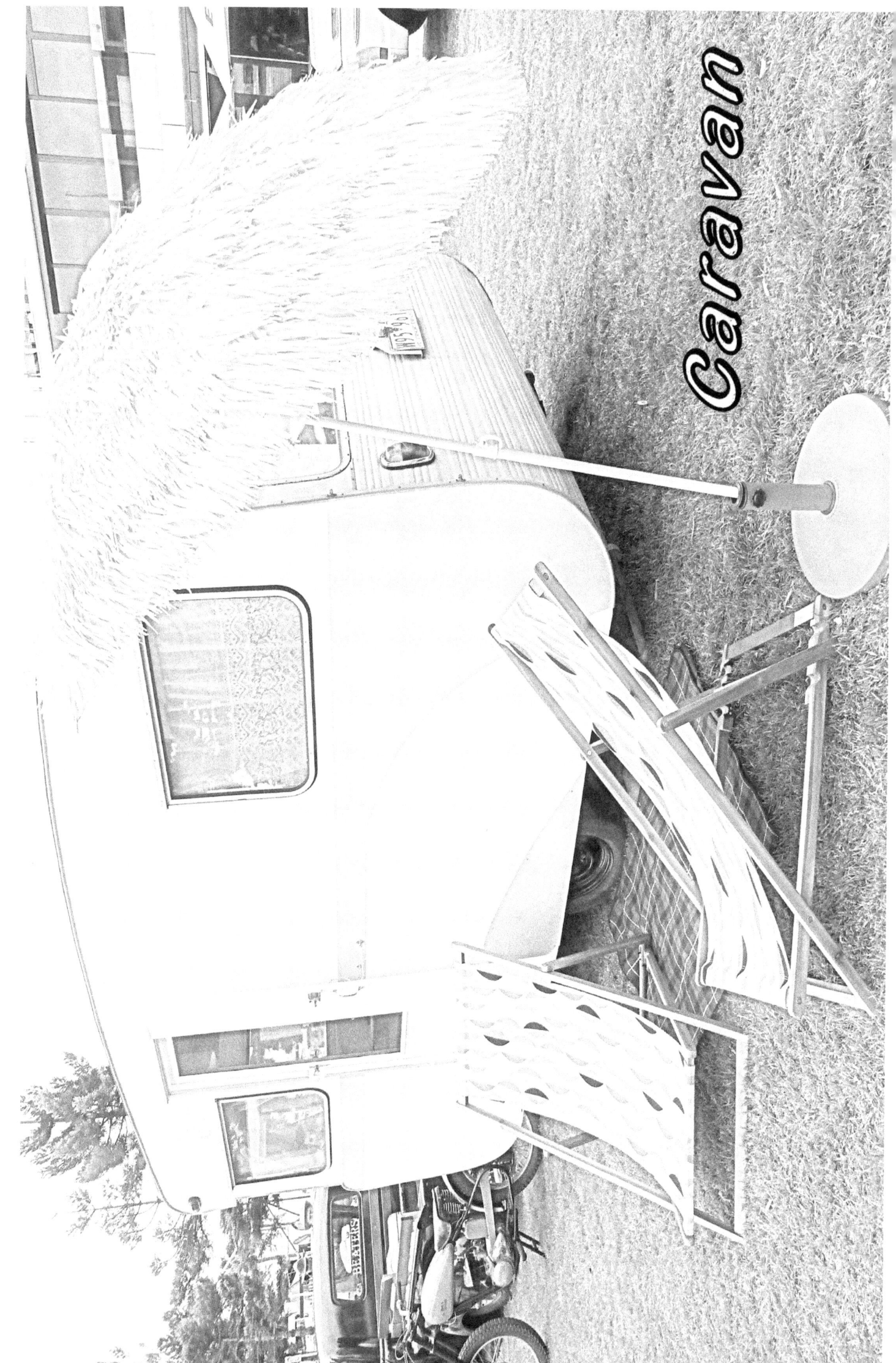

Caravan

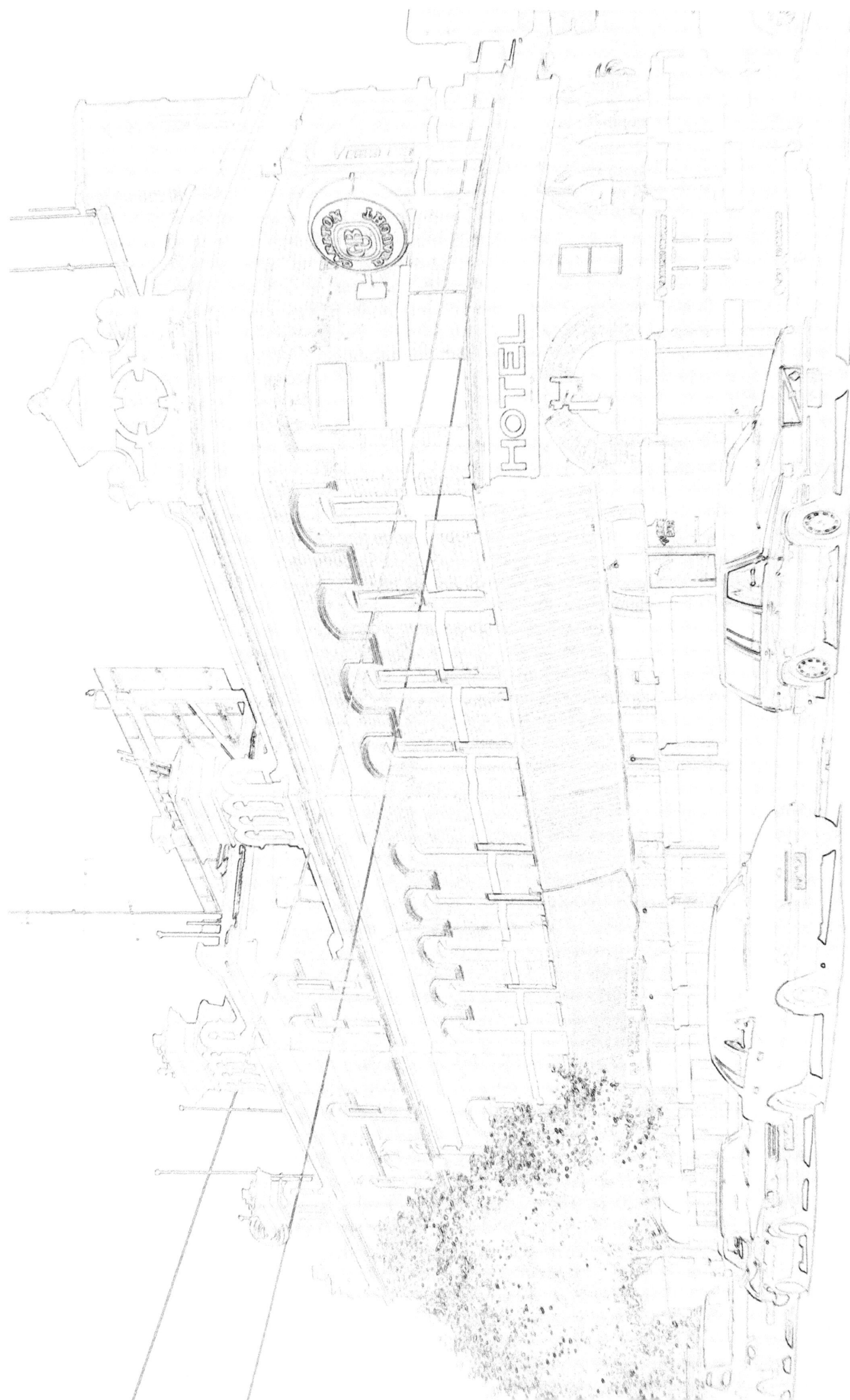

# Cruise Ship

MECHANICS' INSTITUTE & FREE LIBRARY

SOUTHSEA
OIL COMPANY
LAMPS, CHIMNEYS
& GLOBES
MACHINERY OIL
LAMP OIL NAPHTHA

SWAMP WATER

SOUTHSEA
OIL COMPANY

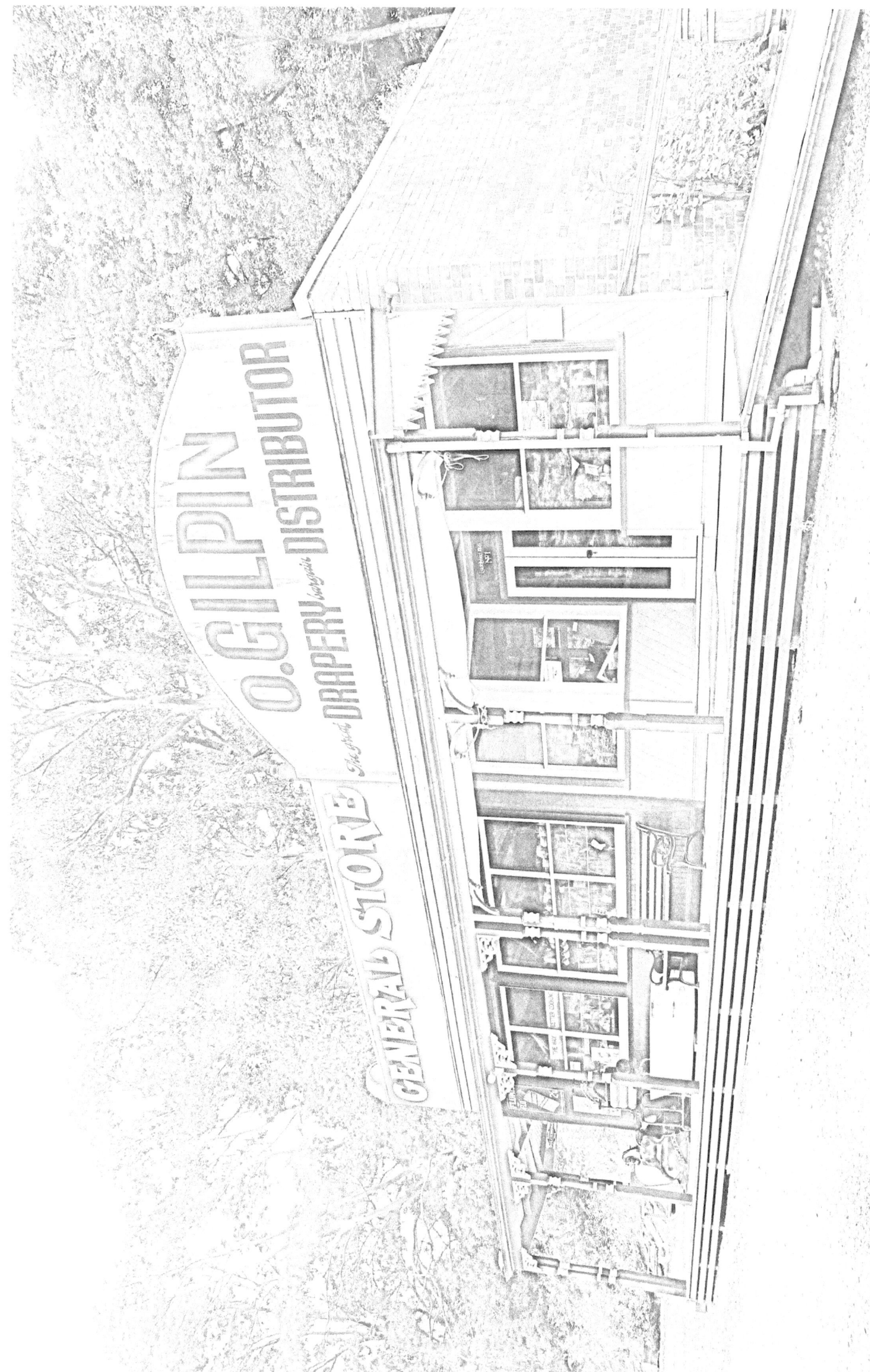

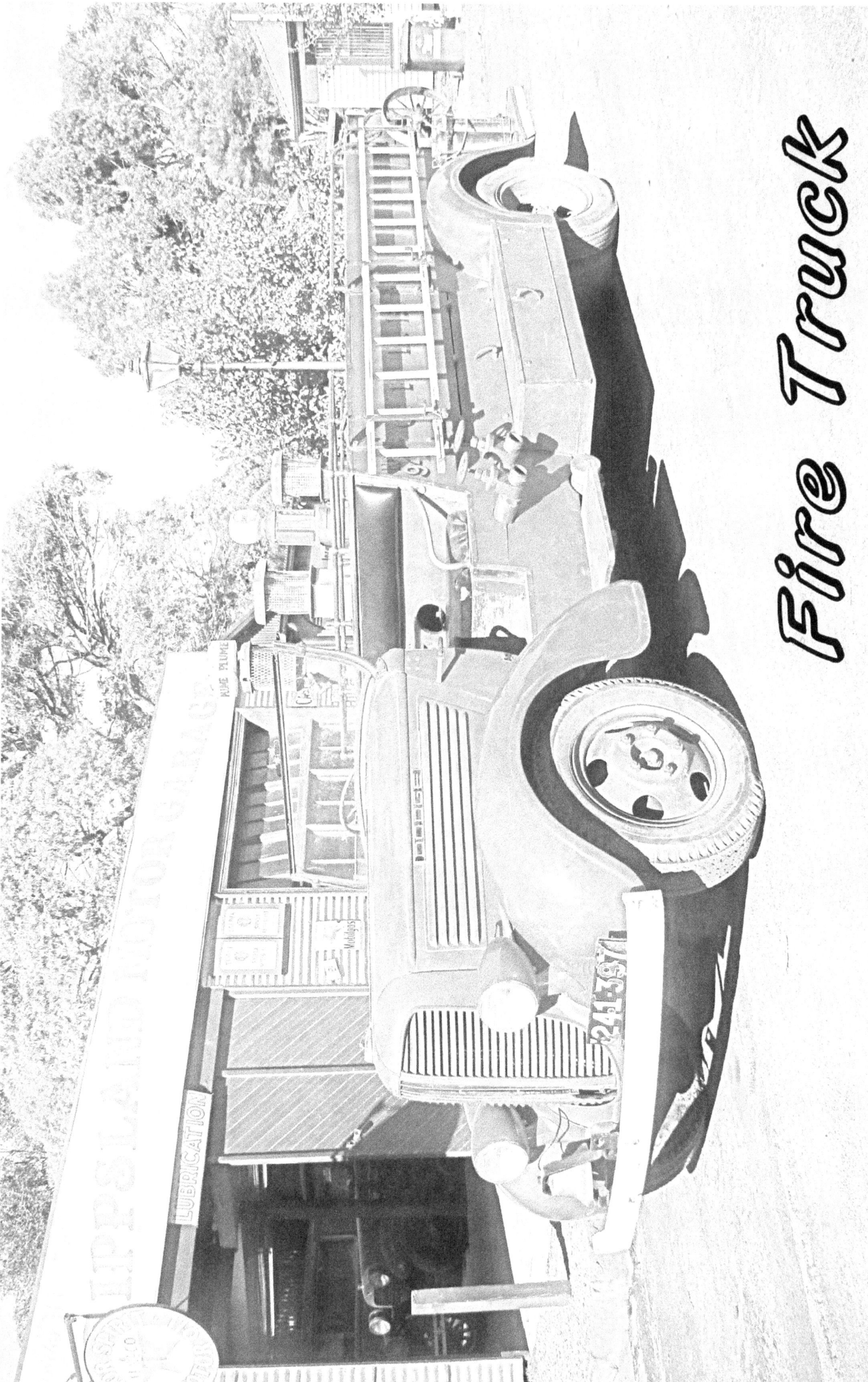

Fire Truck

Flower

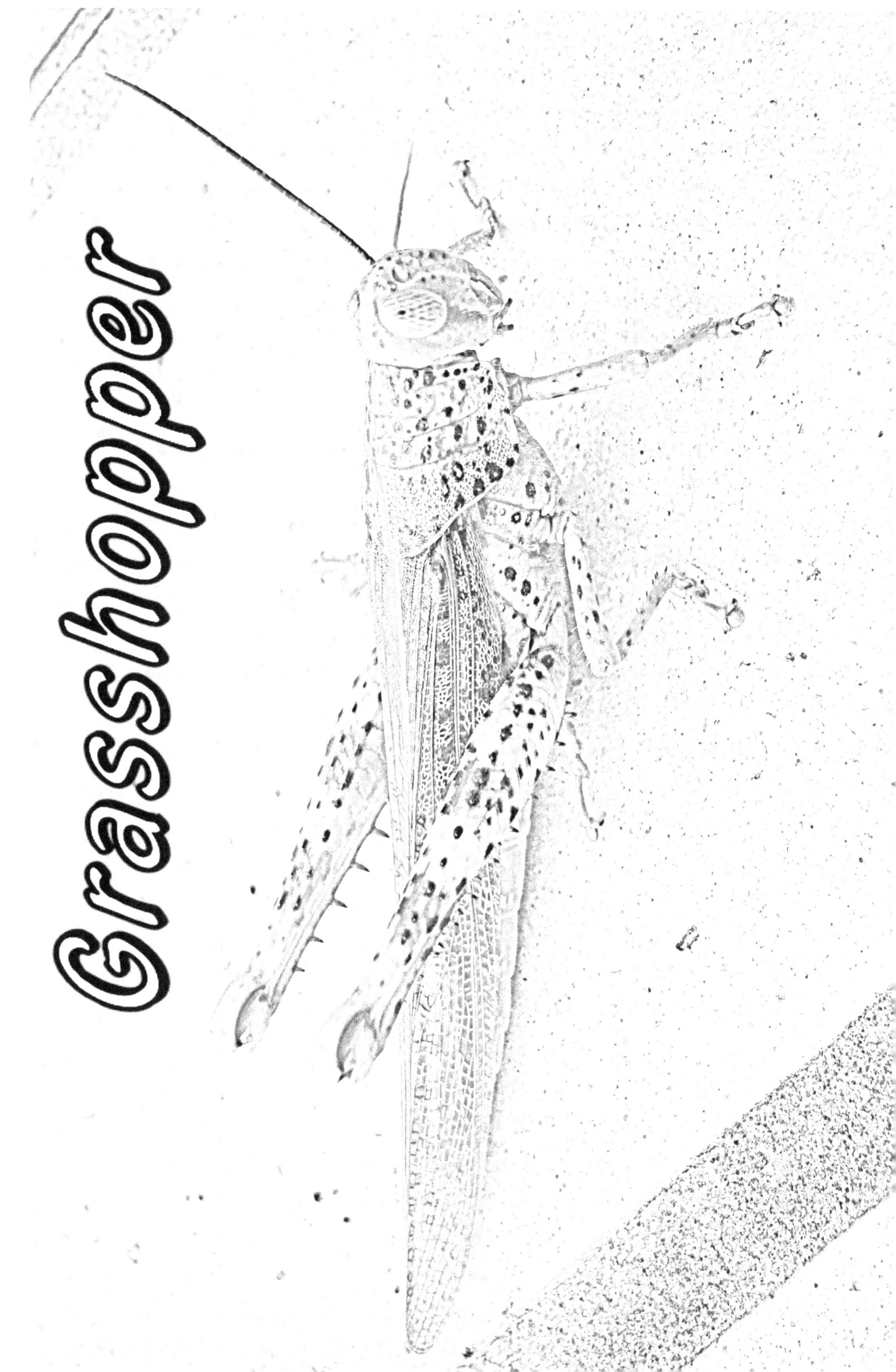

Grasshopper

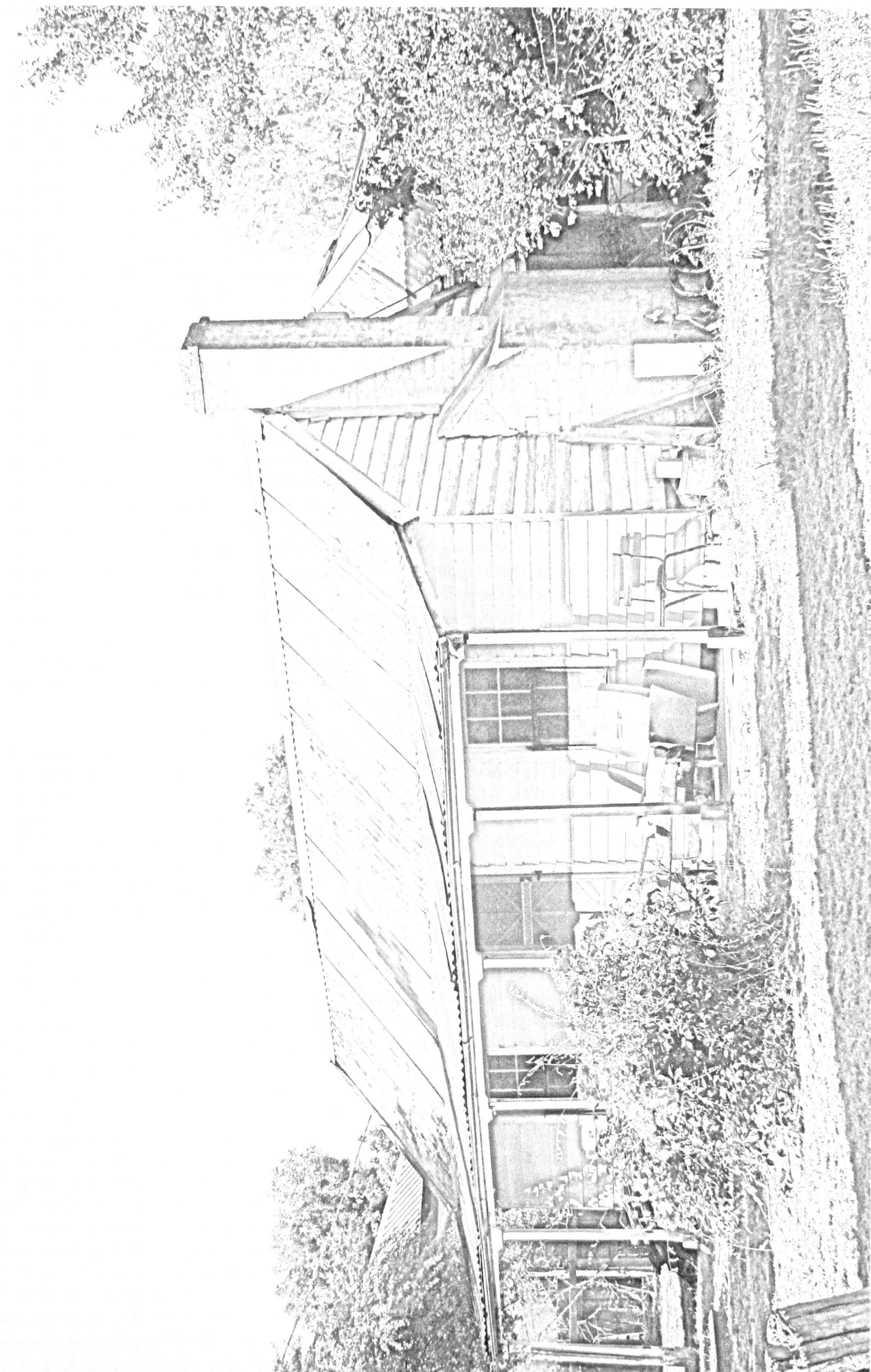

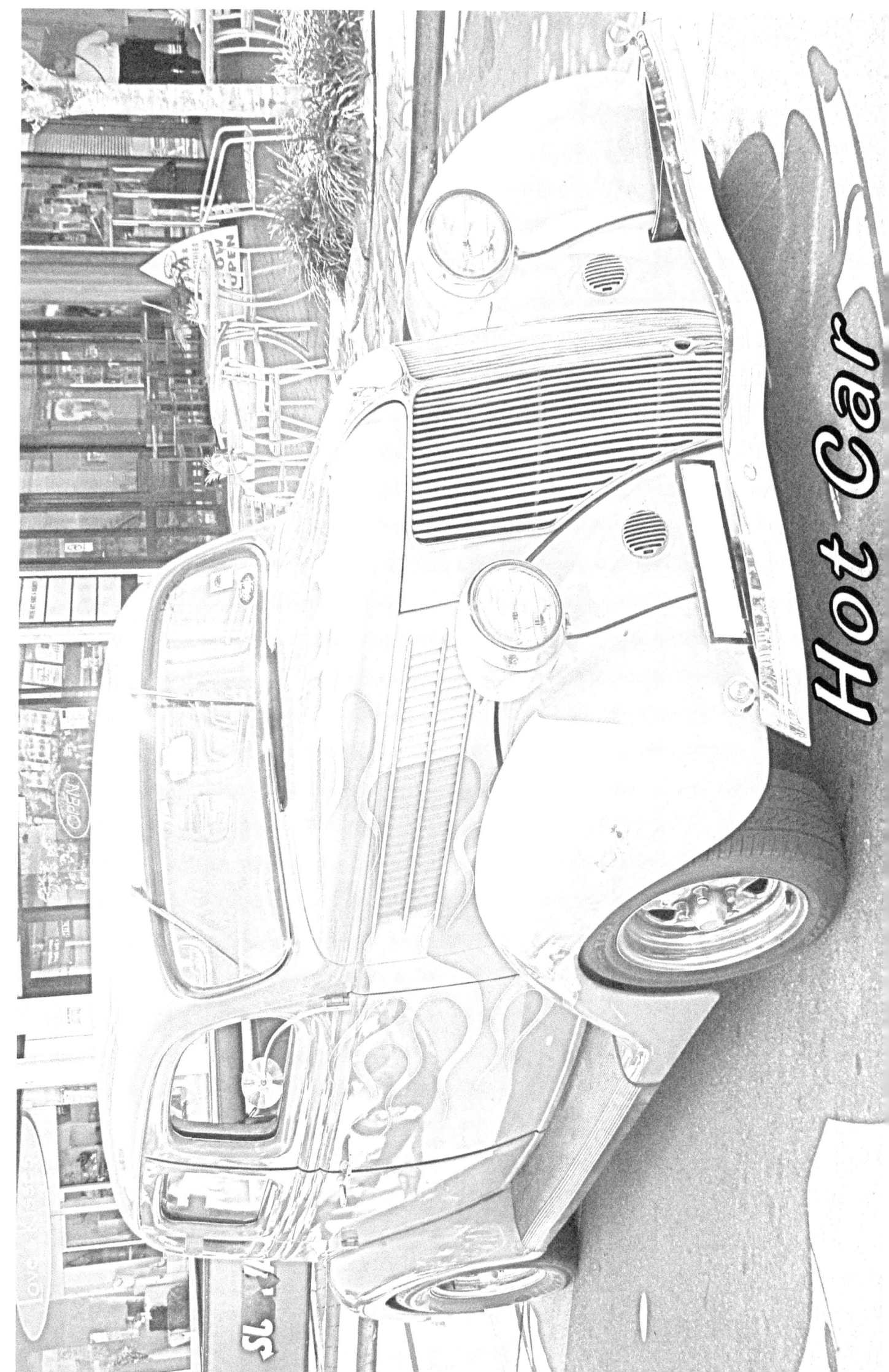

Hot Car

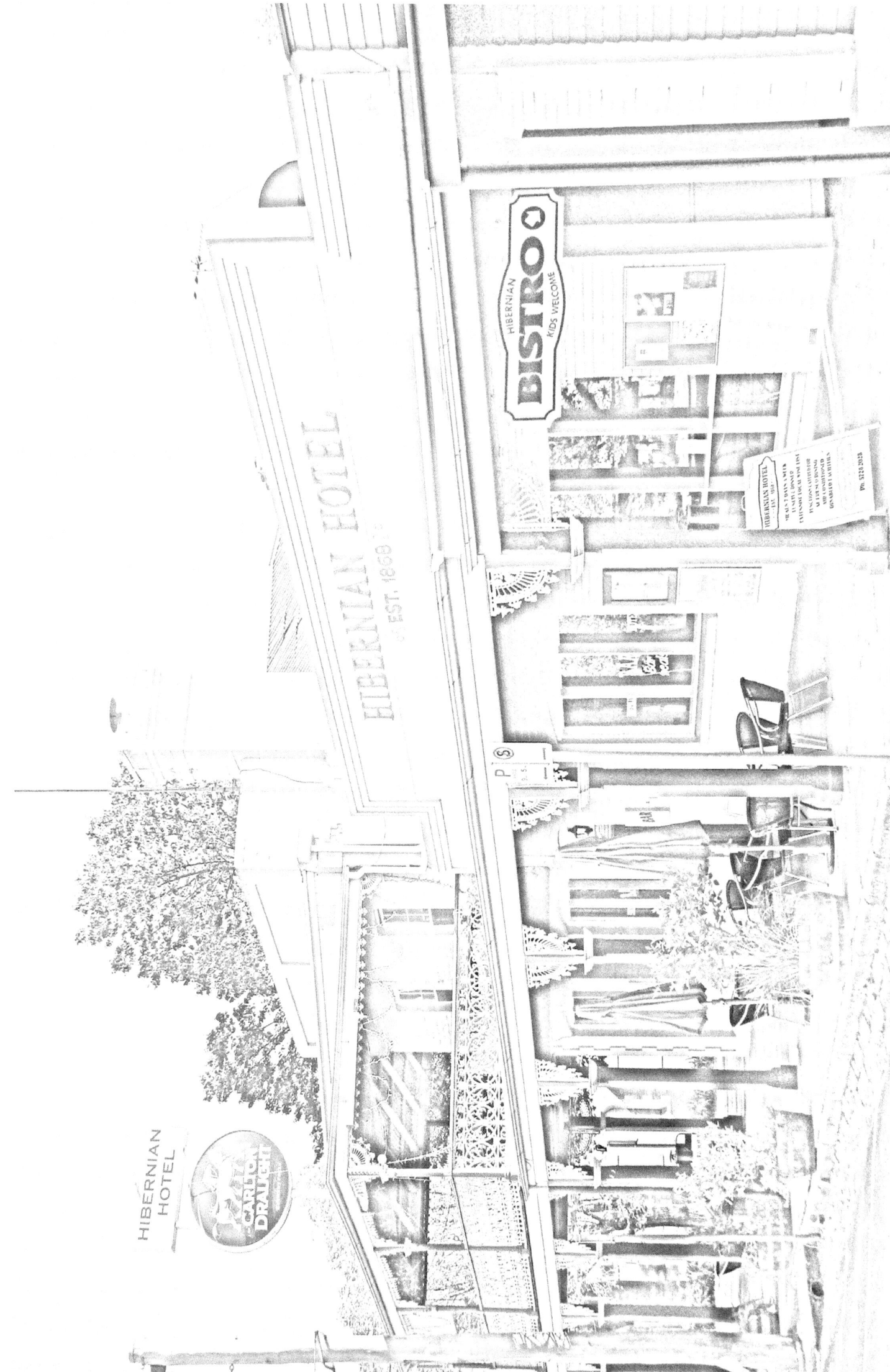

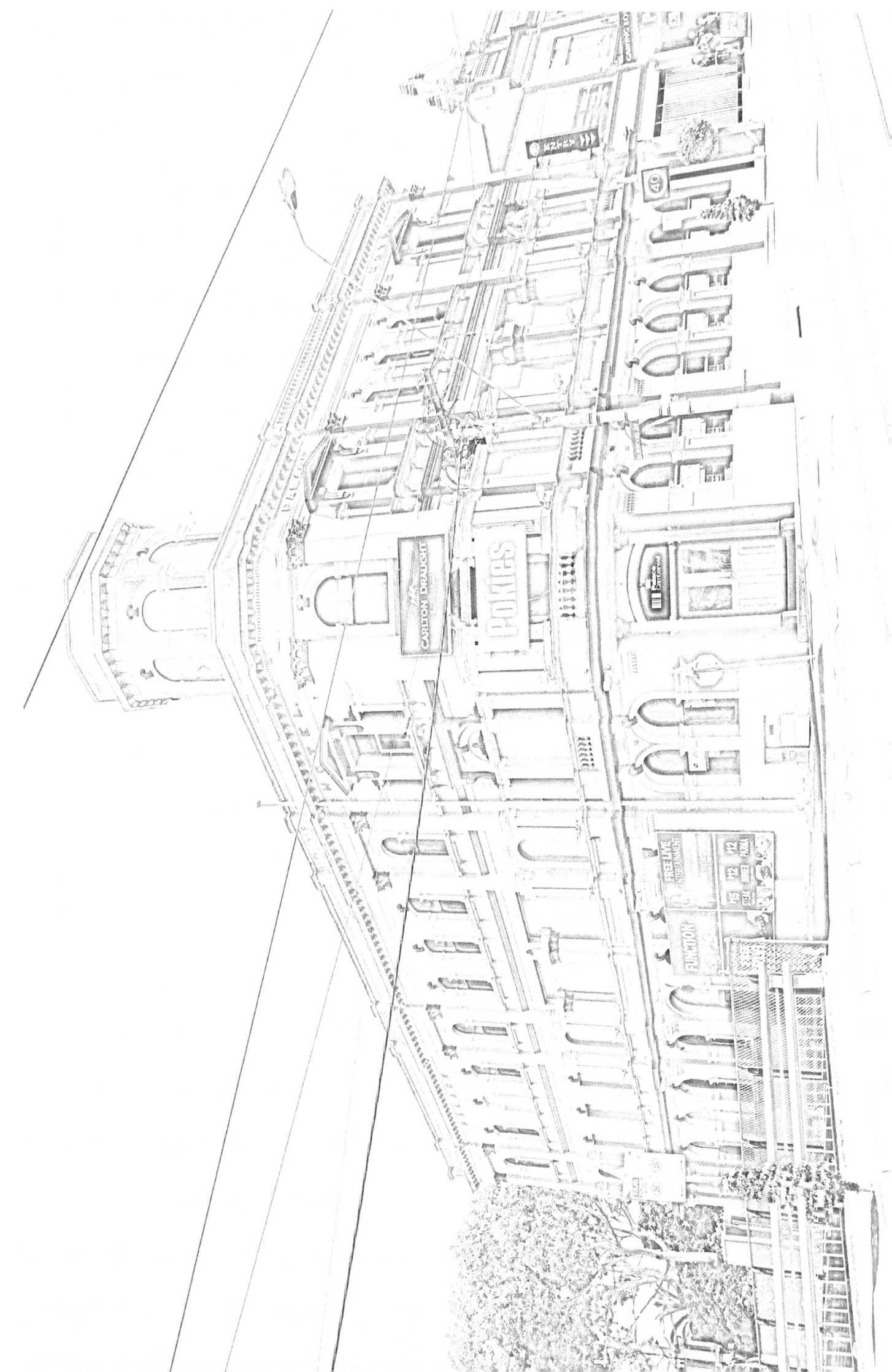

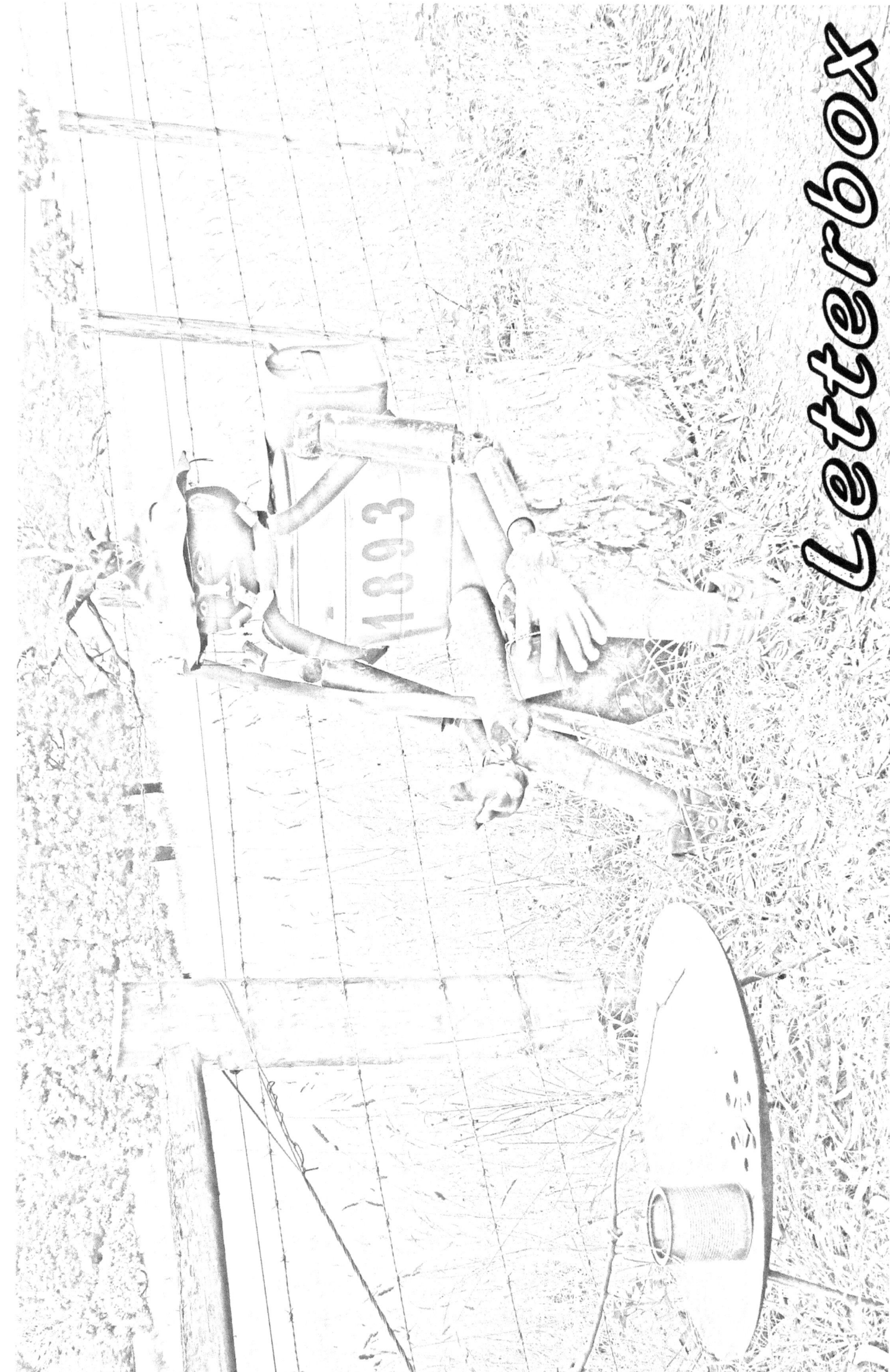

Letterbox

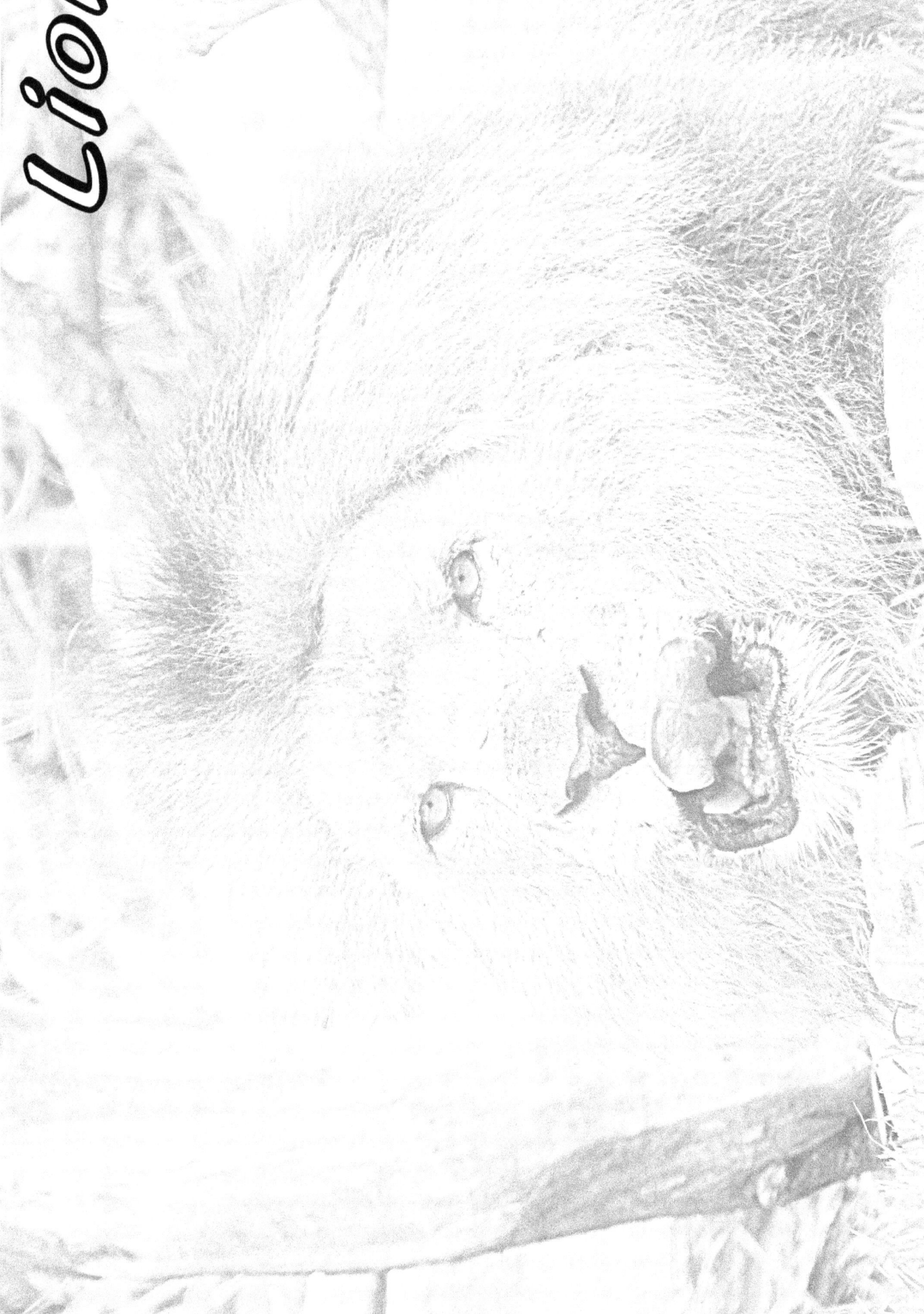

Lion

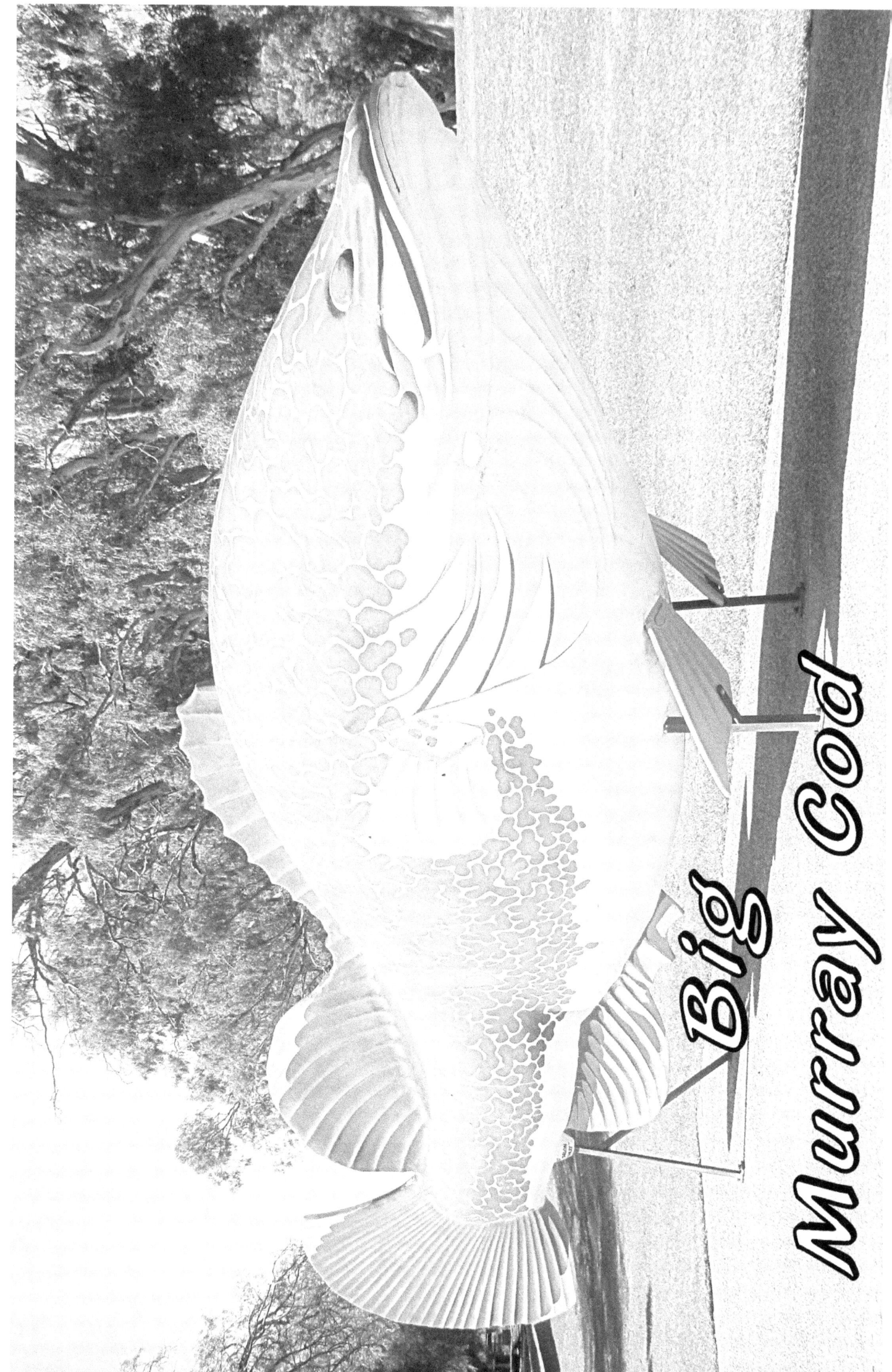

Peacock

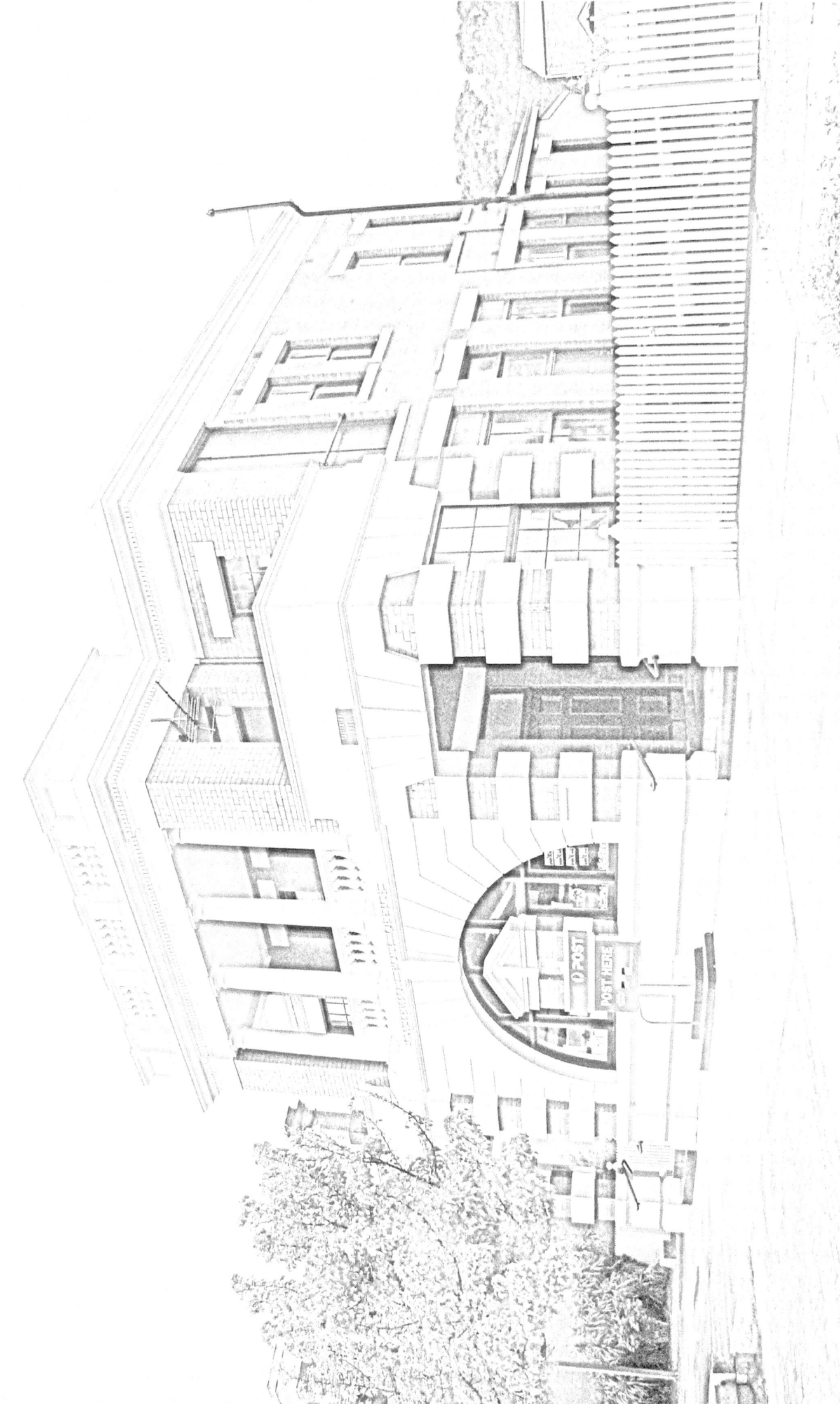

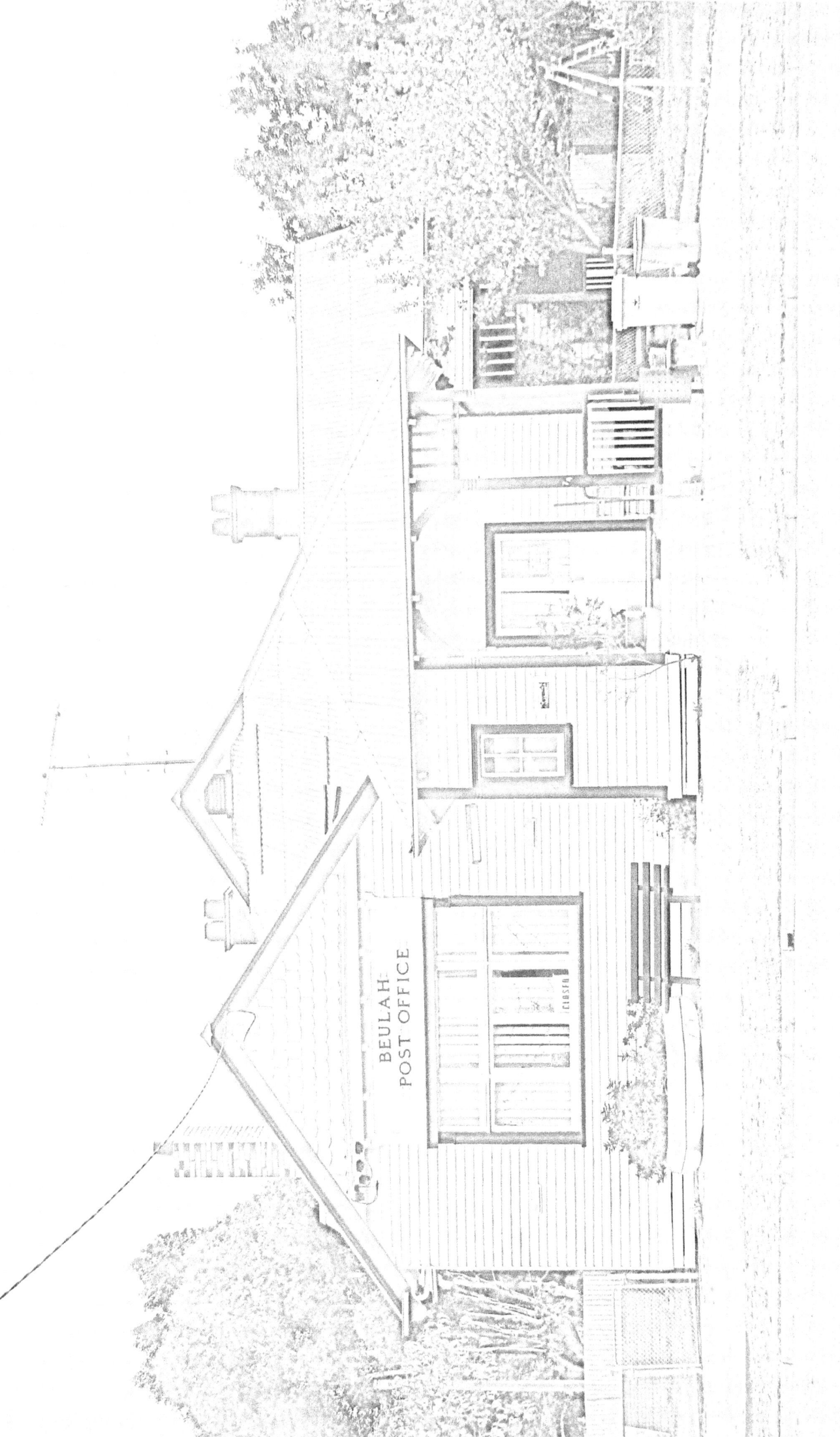

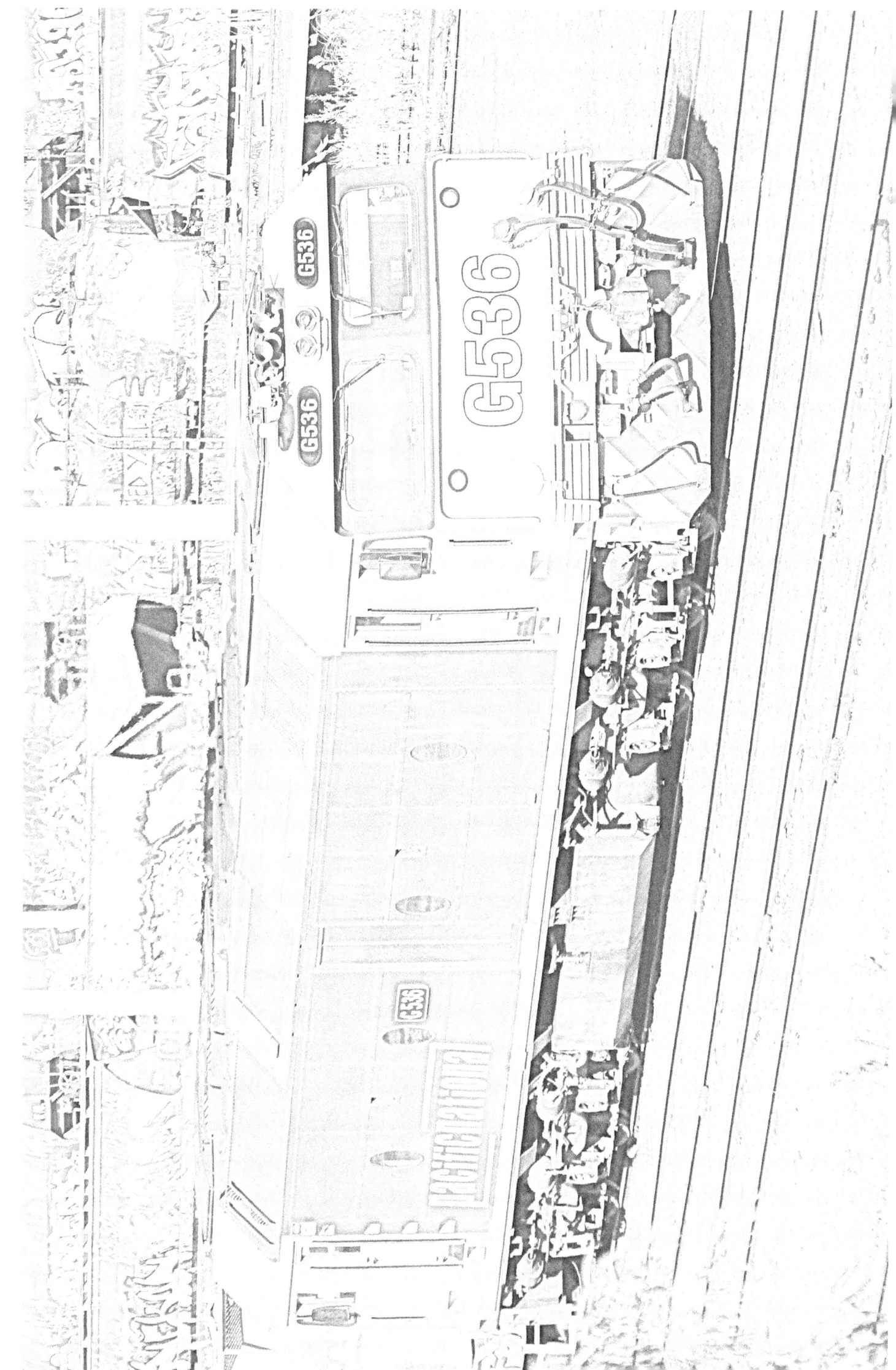

# Sailing Boats

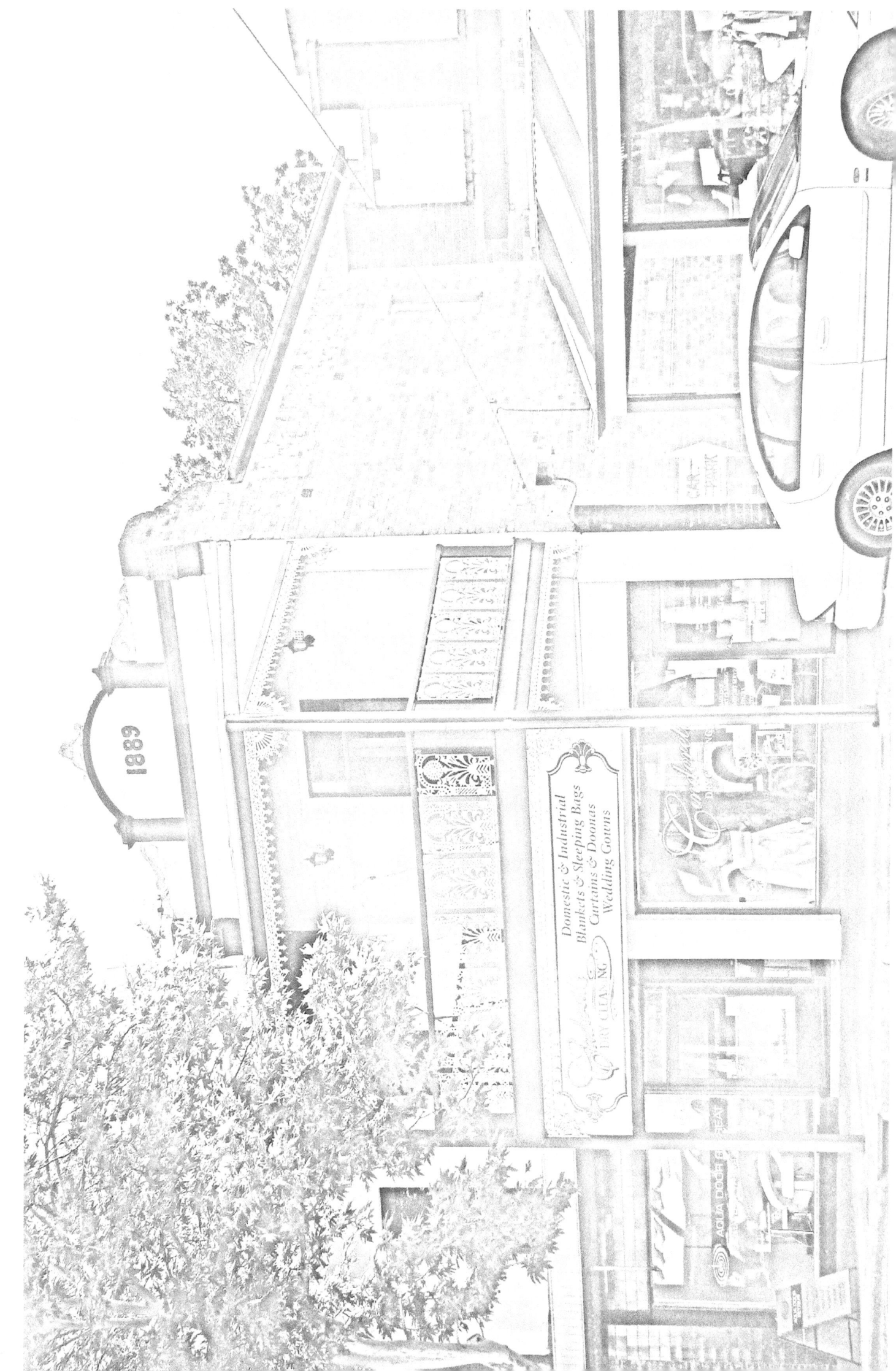

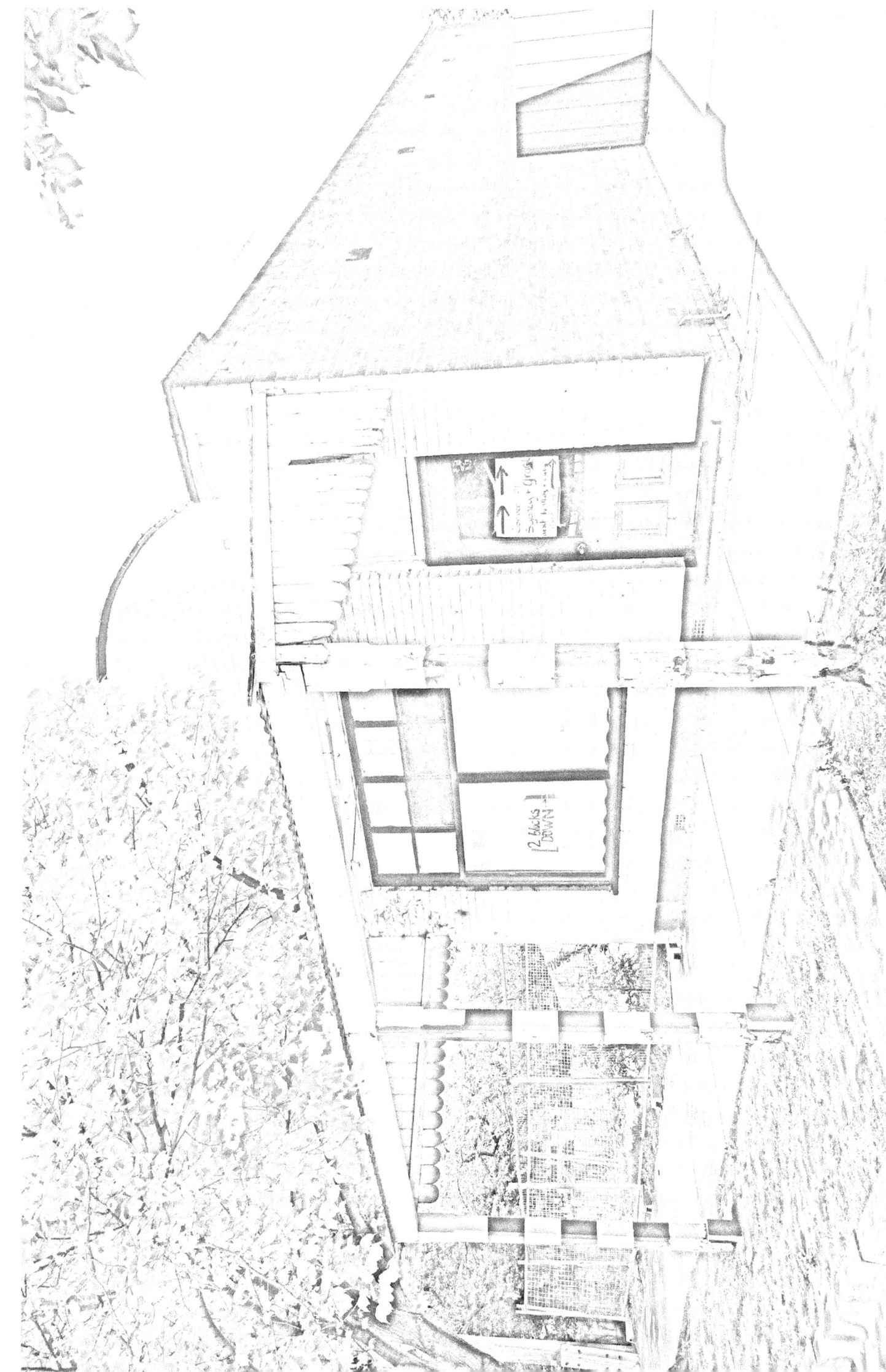

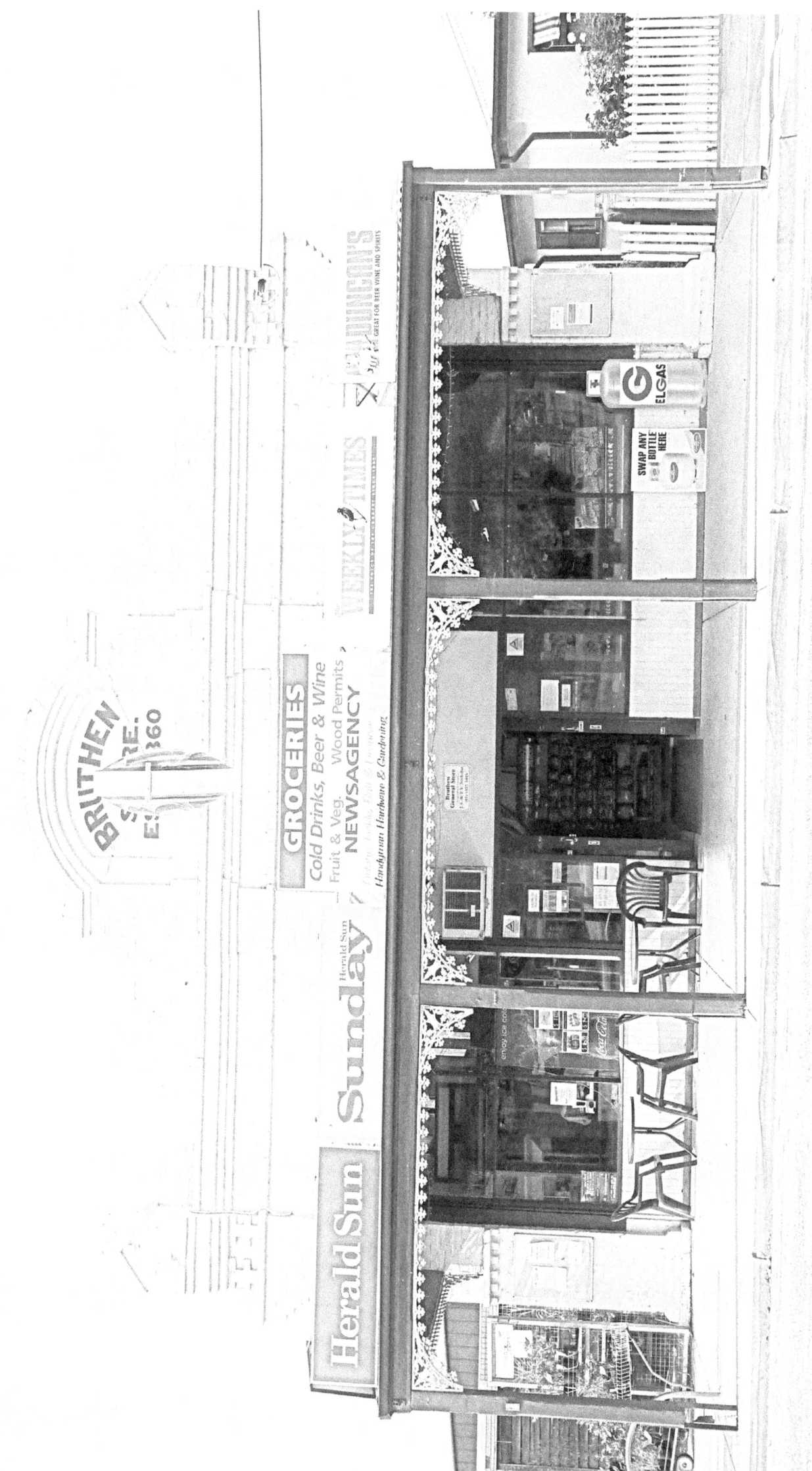

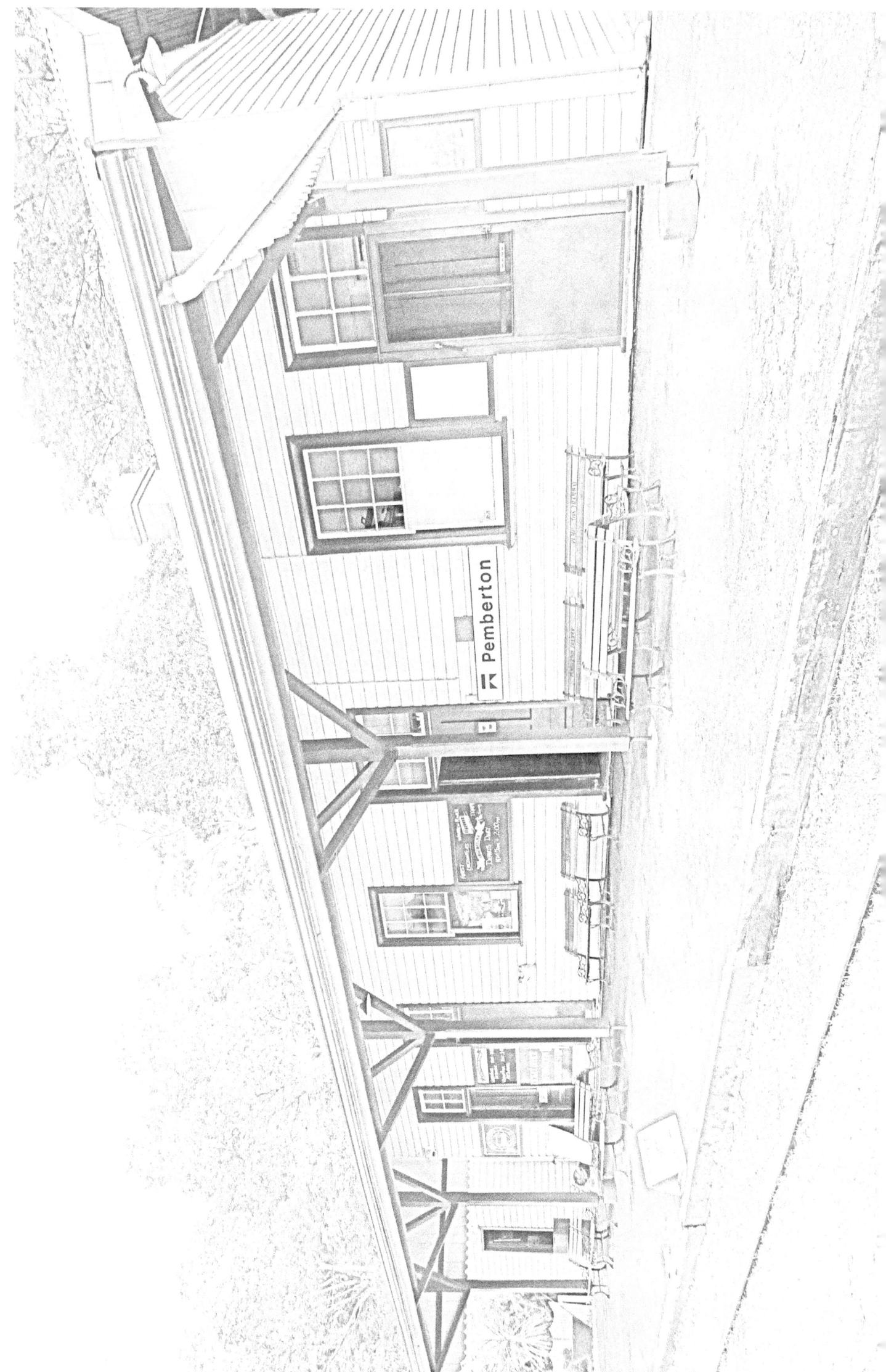

Tiger

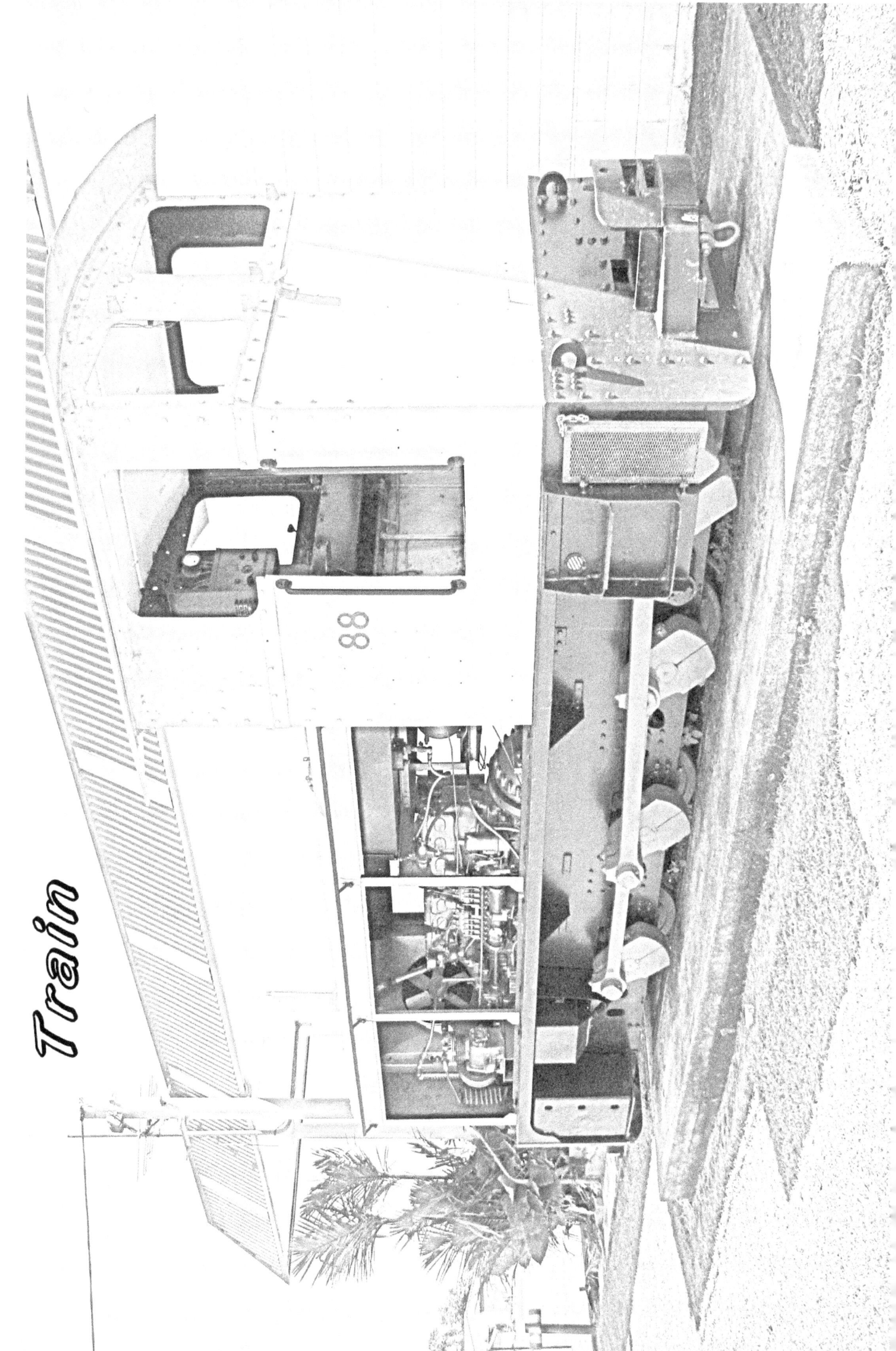

Train

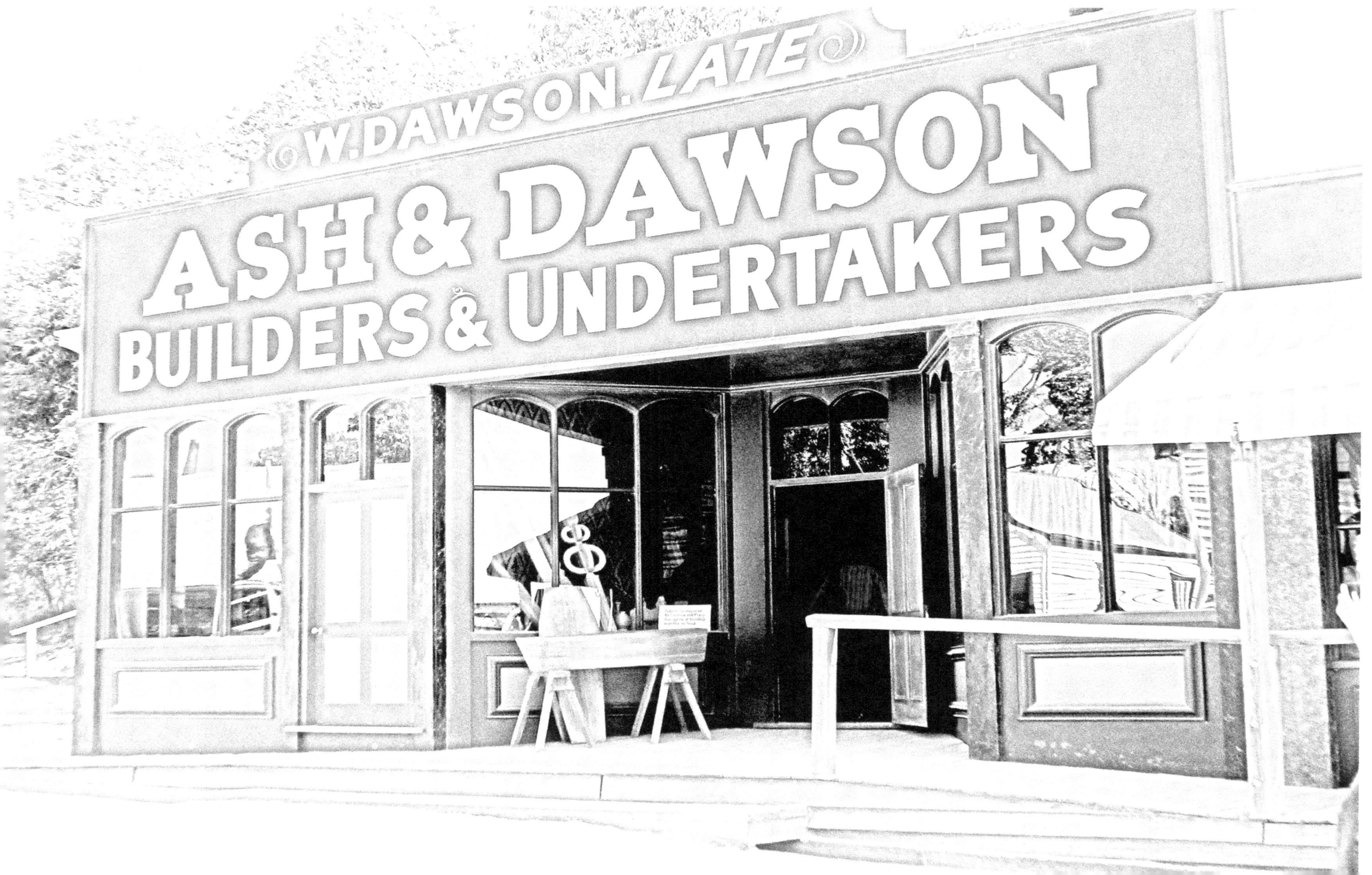
W. DAWSON. LATE
ASH & DAWSON
BUILDERS & UNDERTAKERS

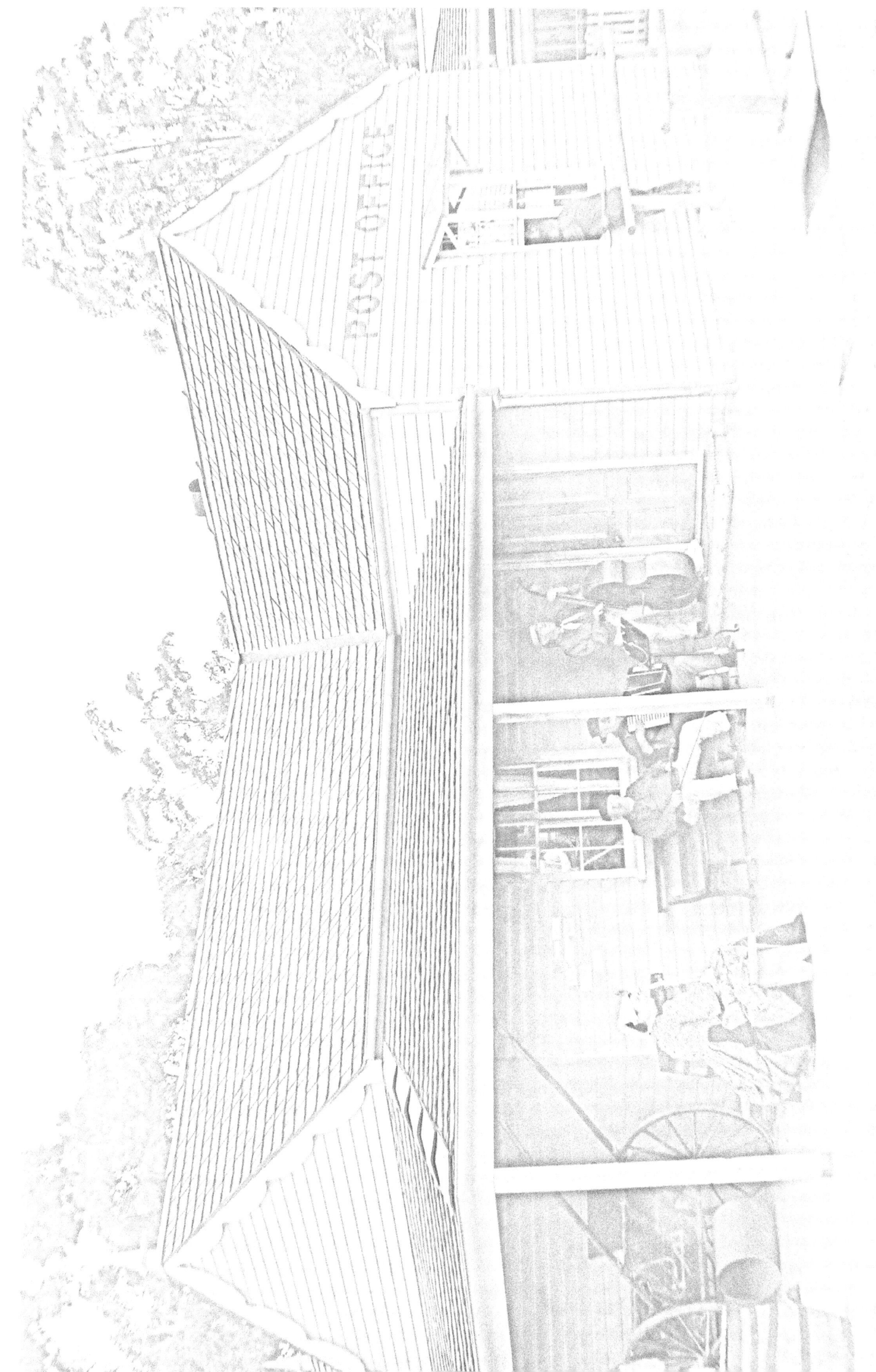

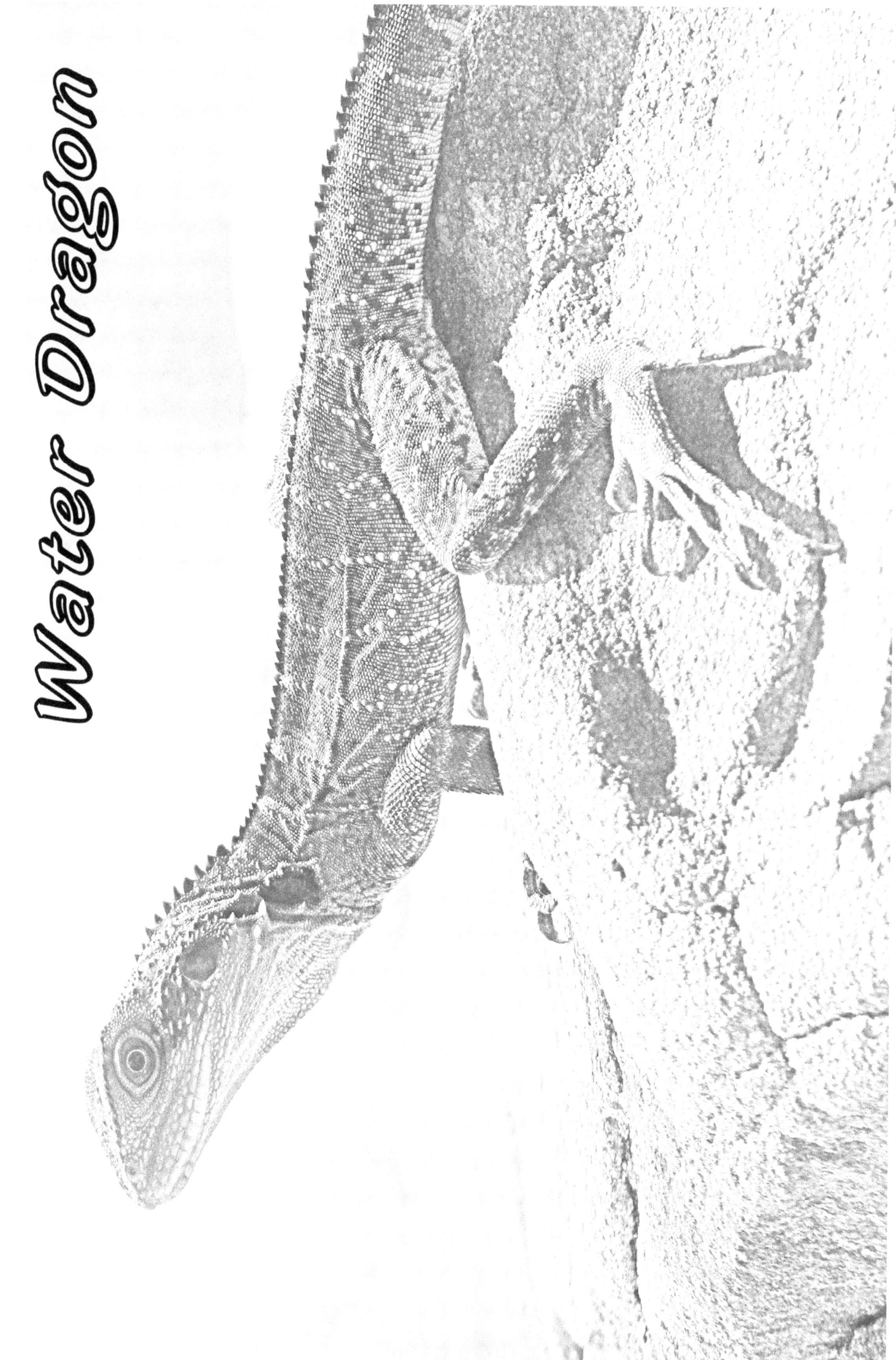

Water Dragon

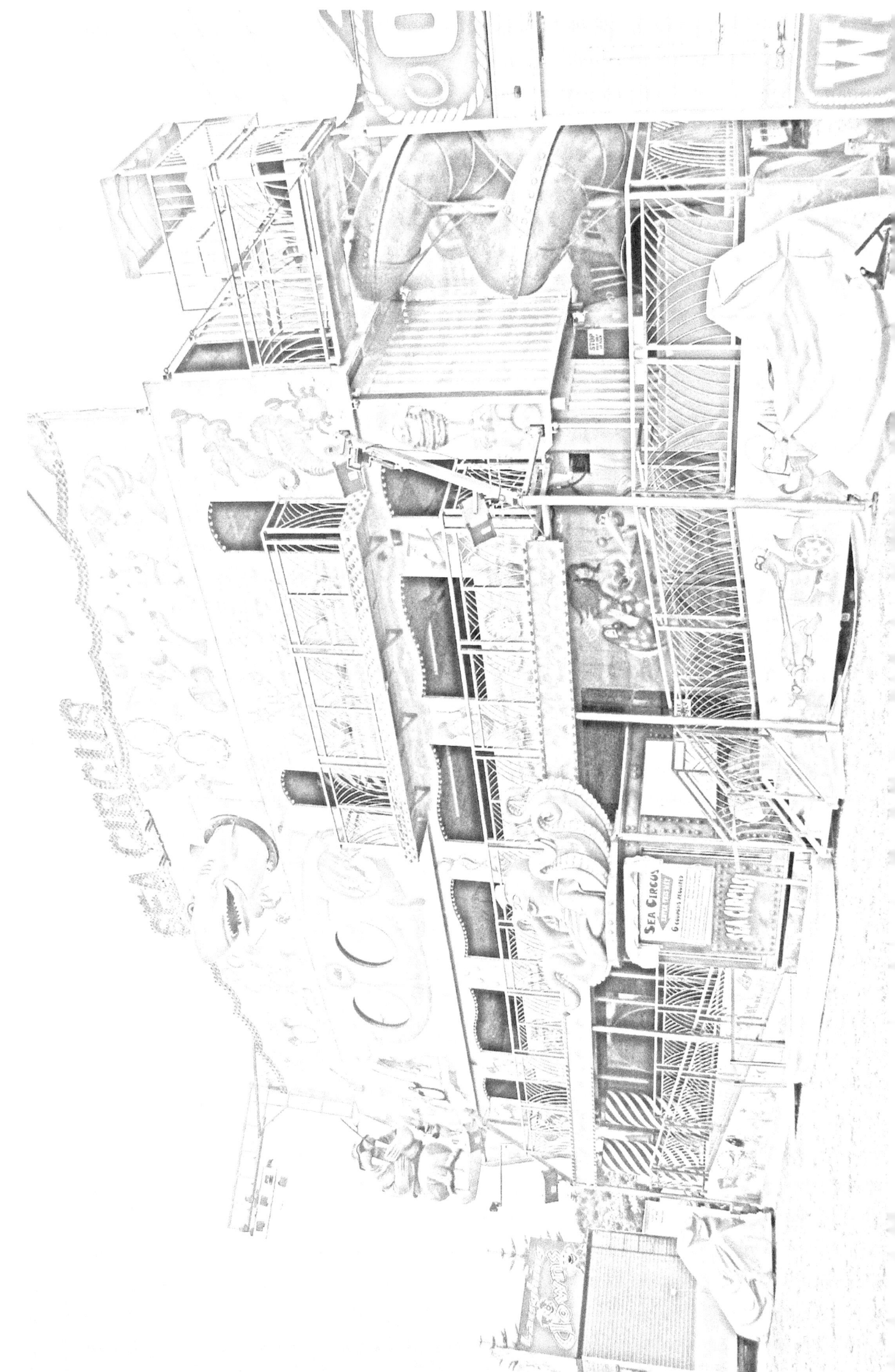

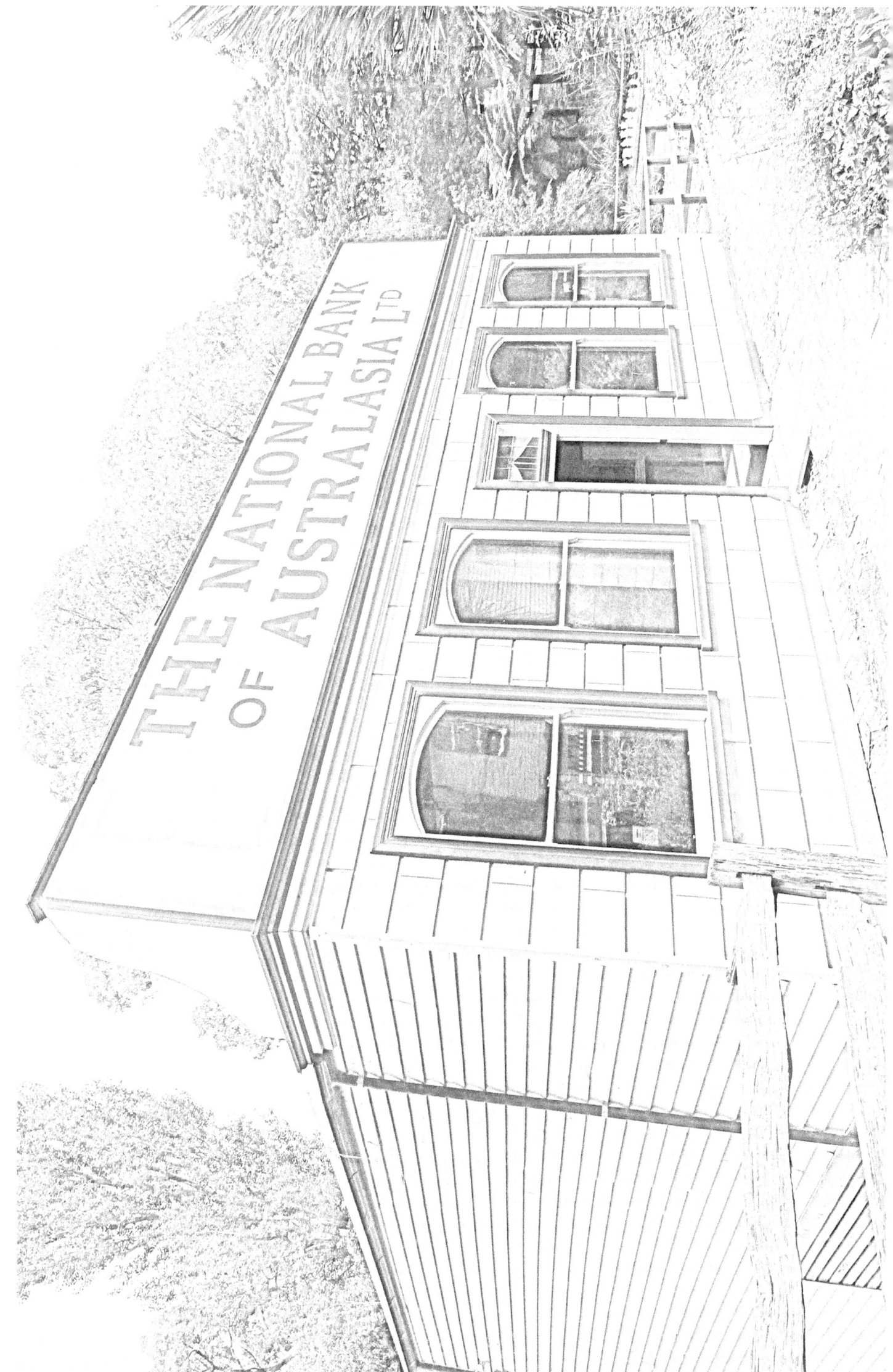

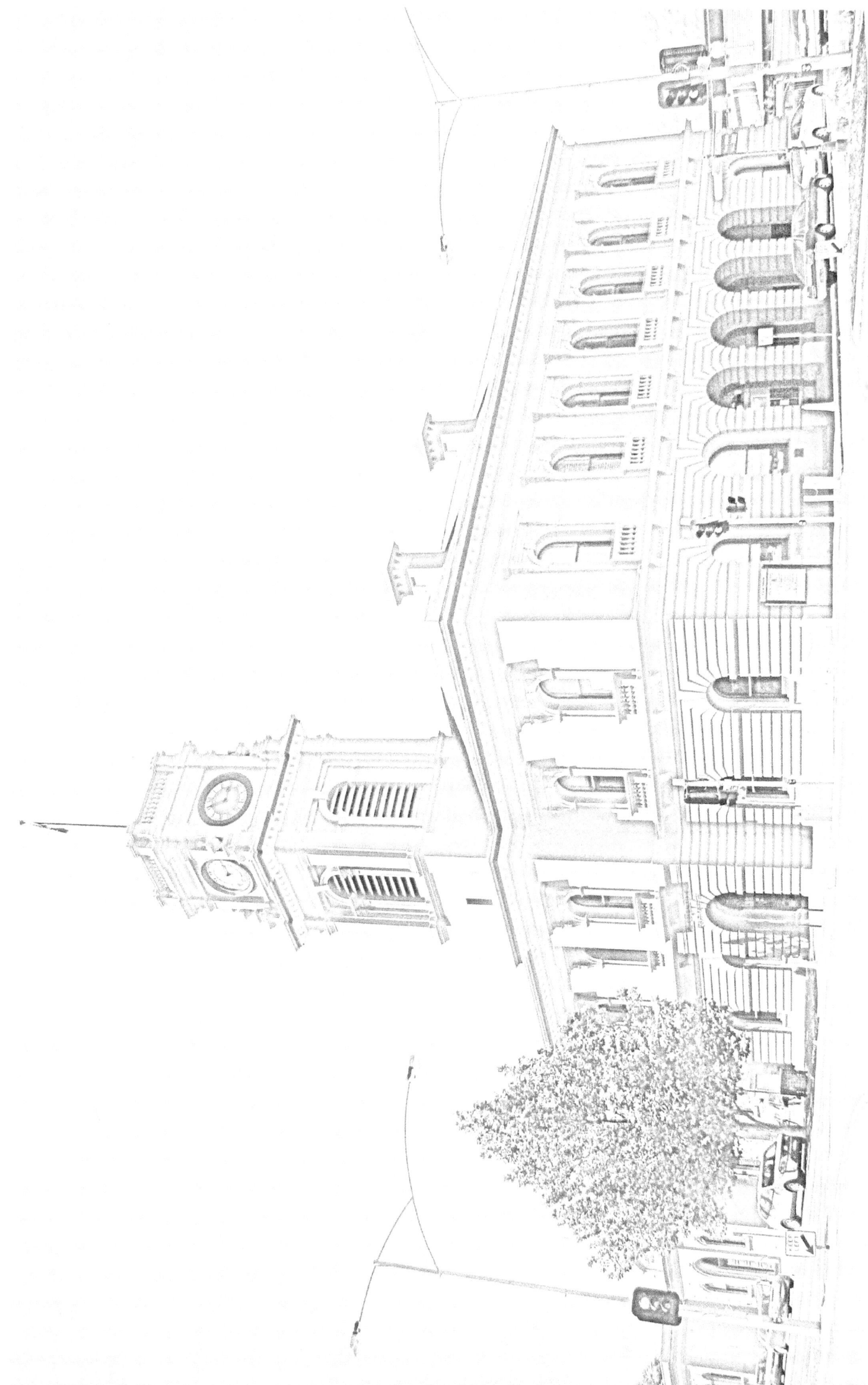

# Big Lobster

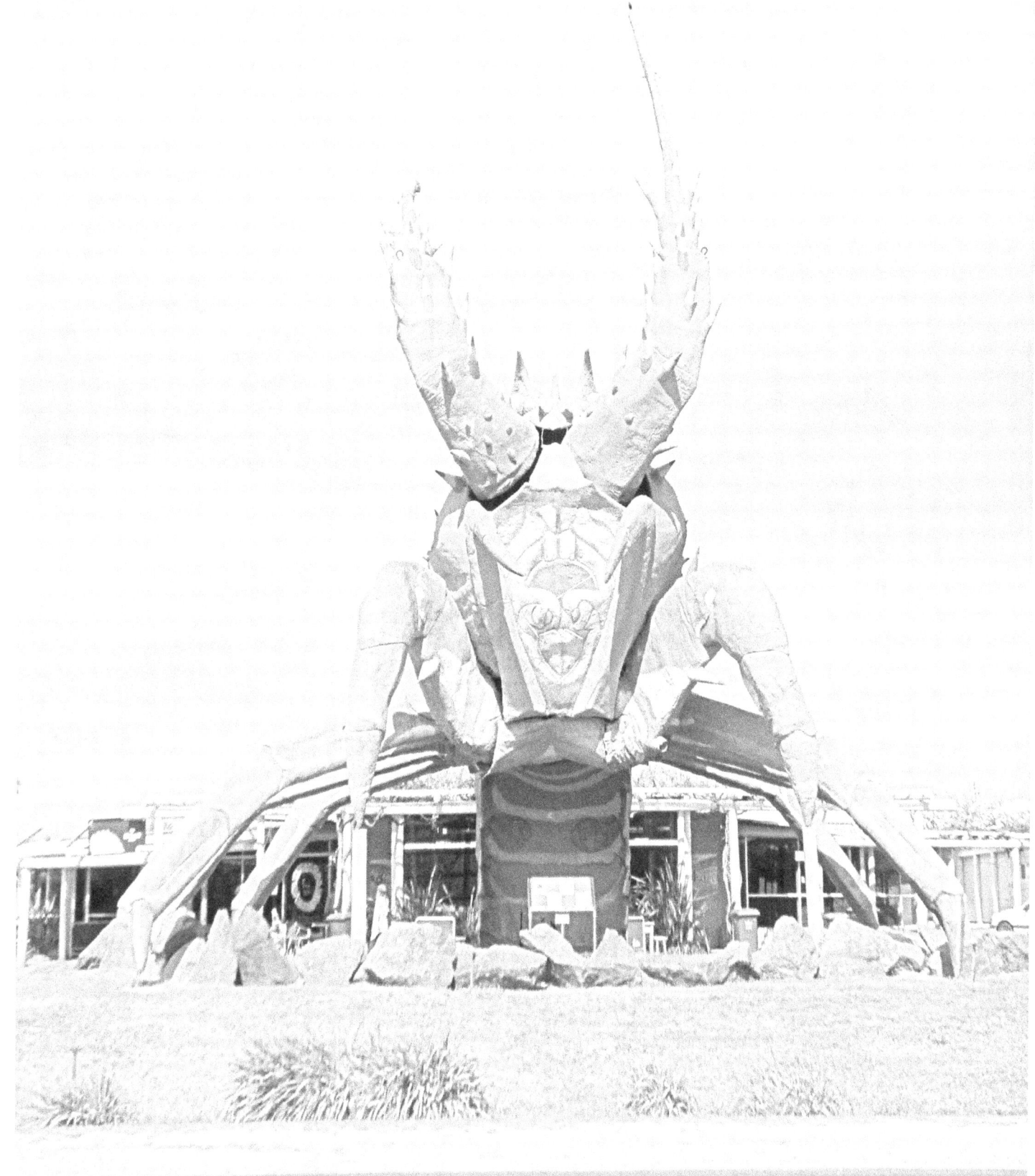

# *Butterfly*

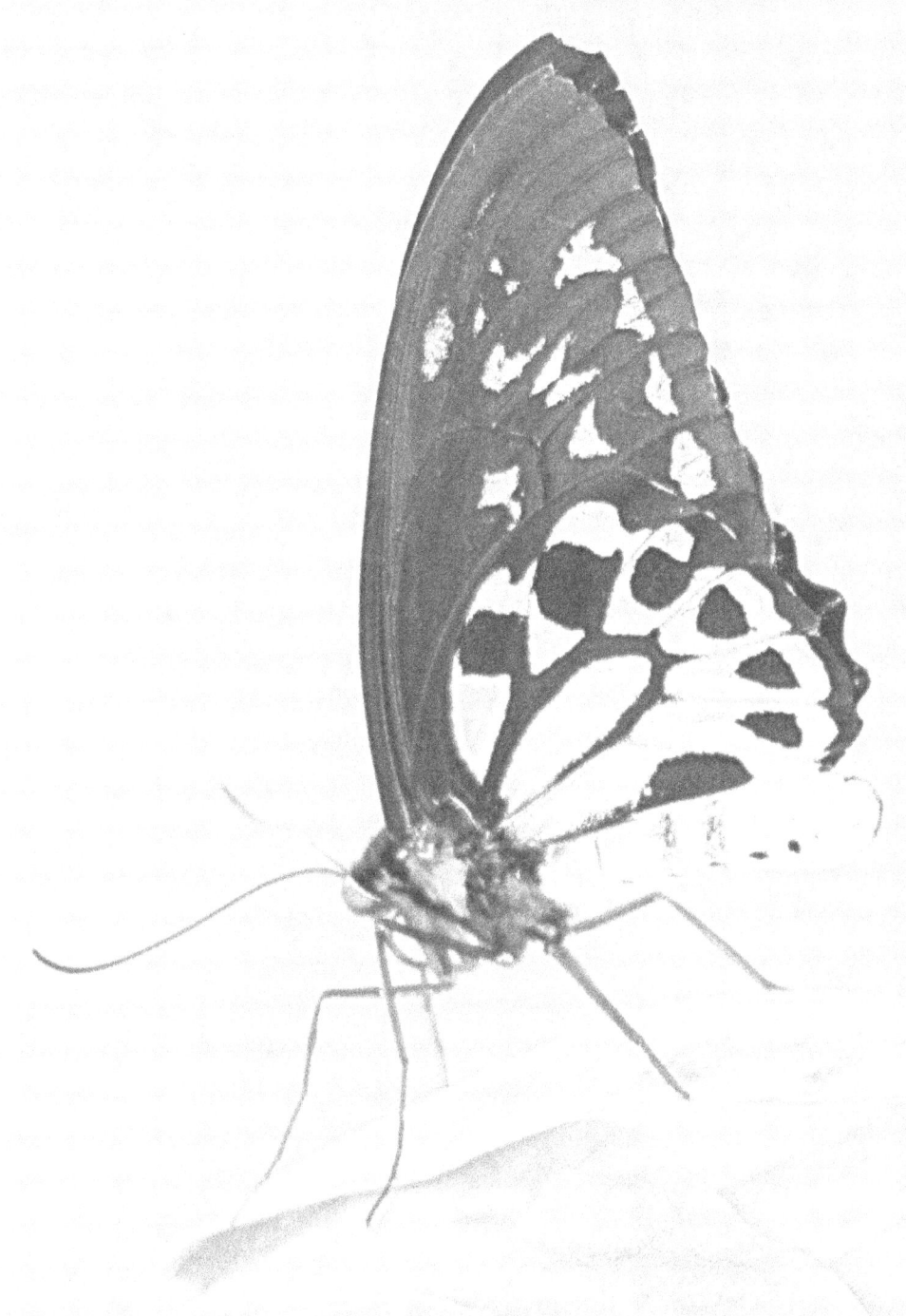

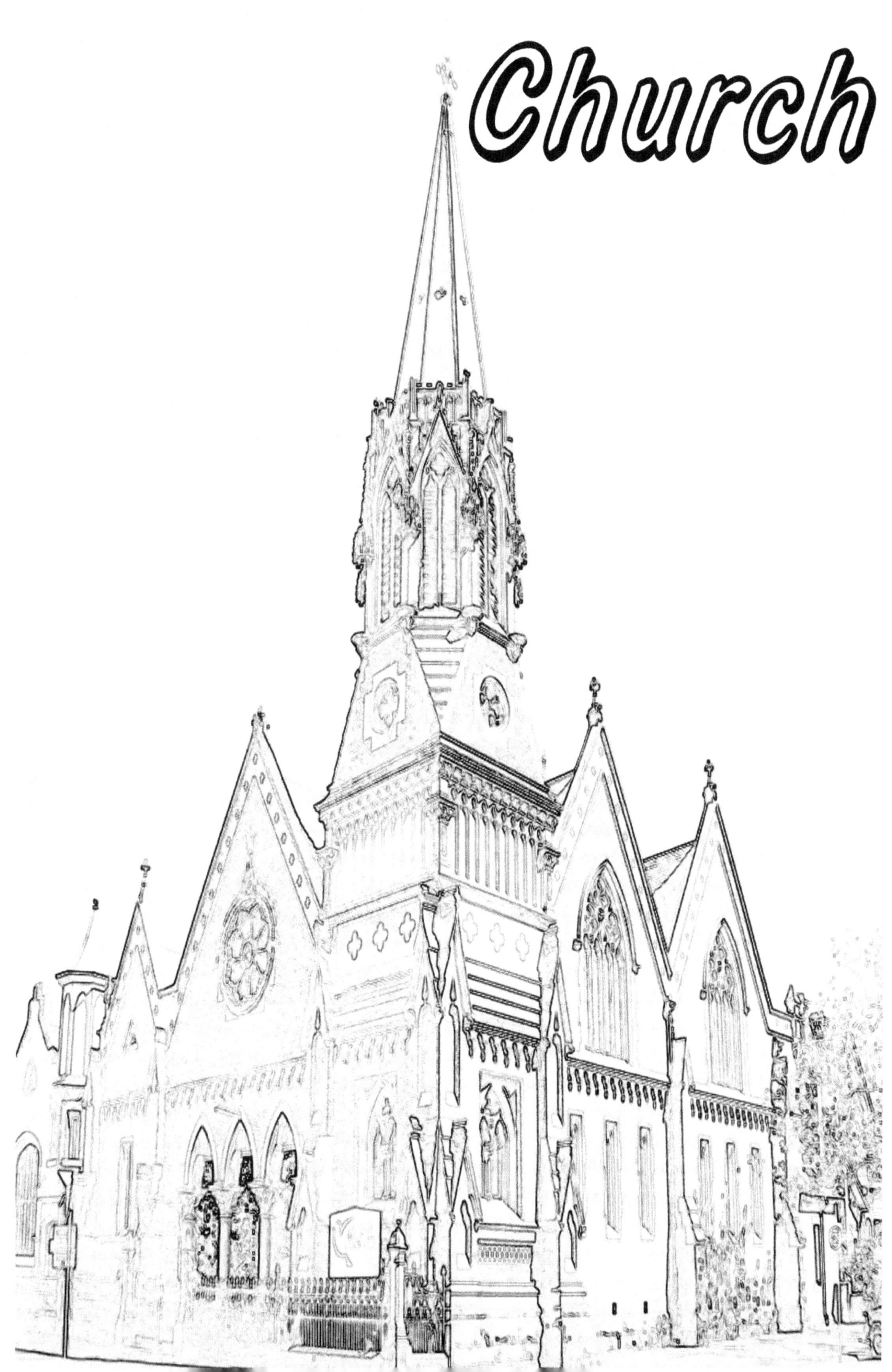

Church

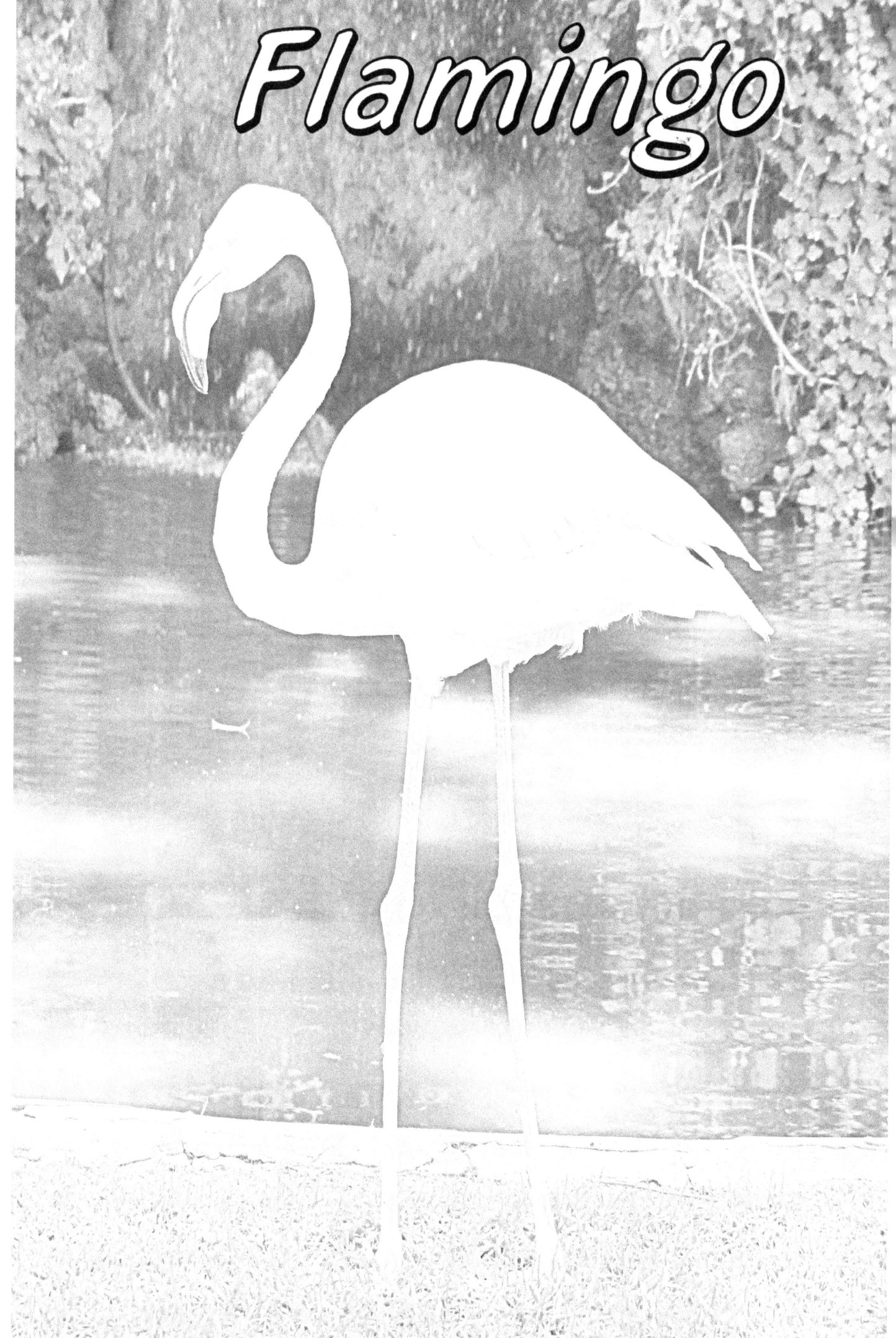

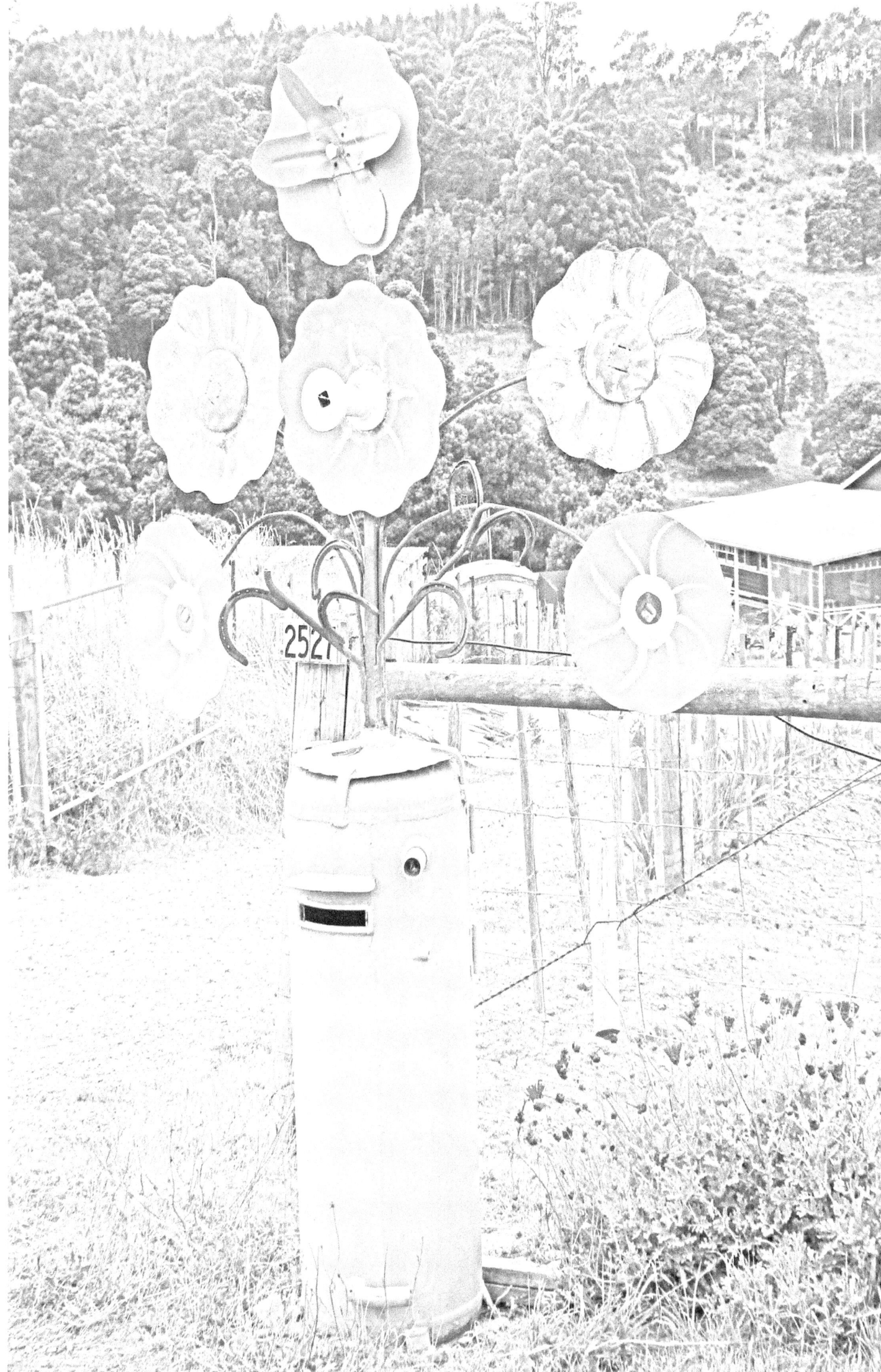

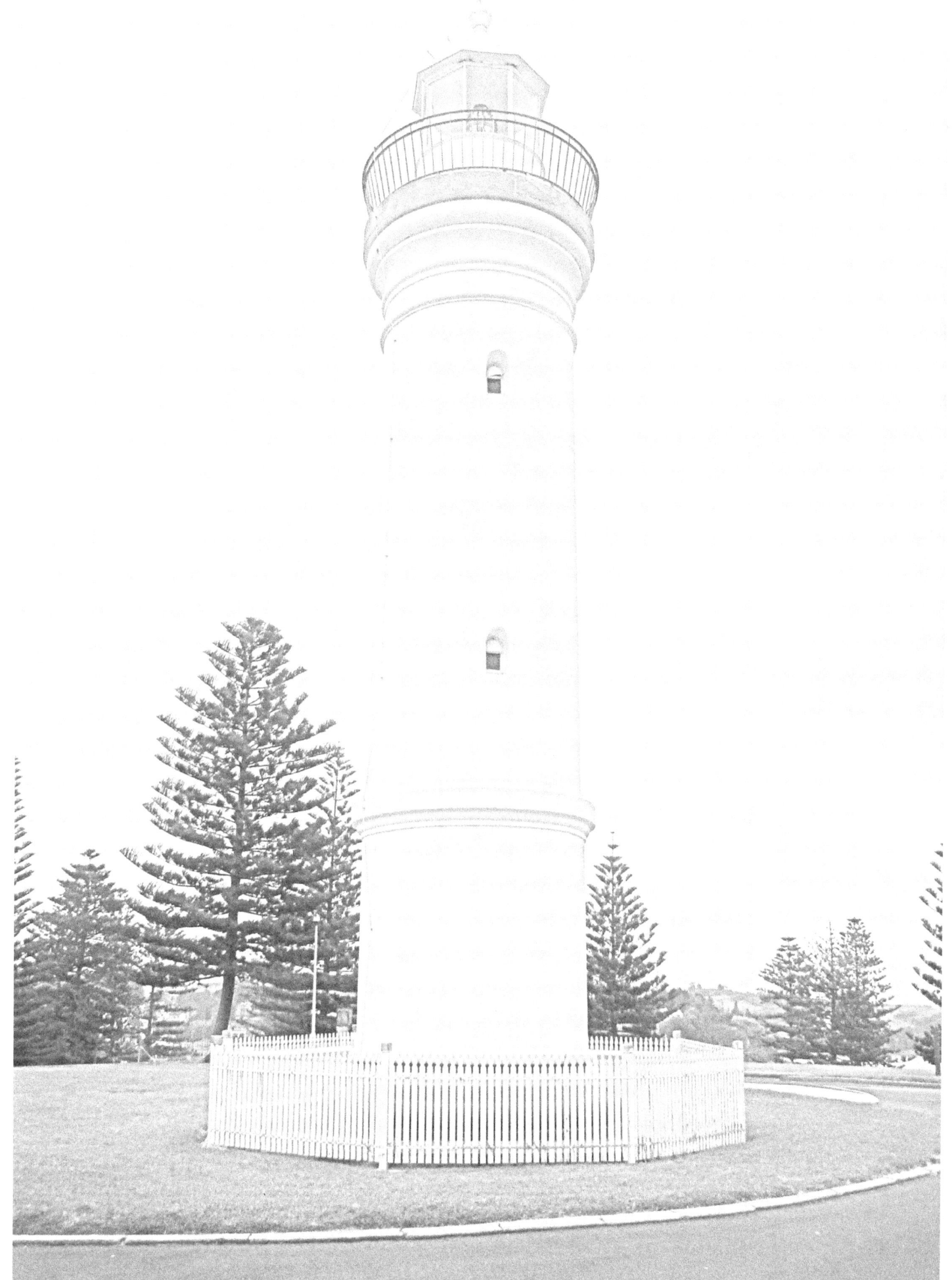

**Lighthouse**

# Mandrill

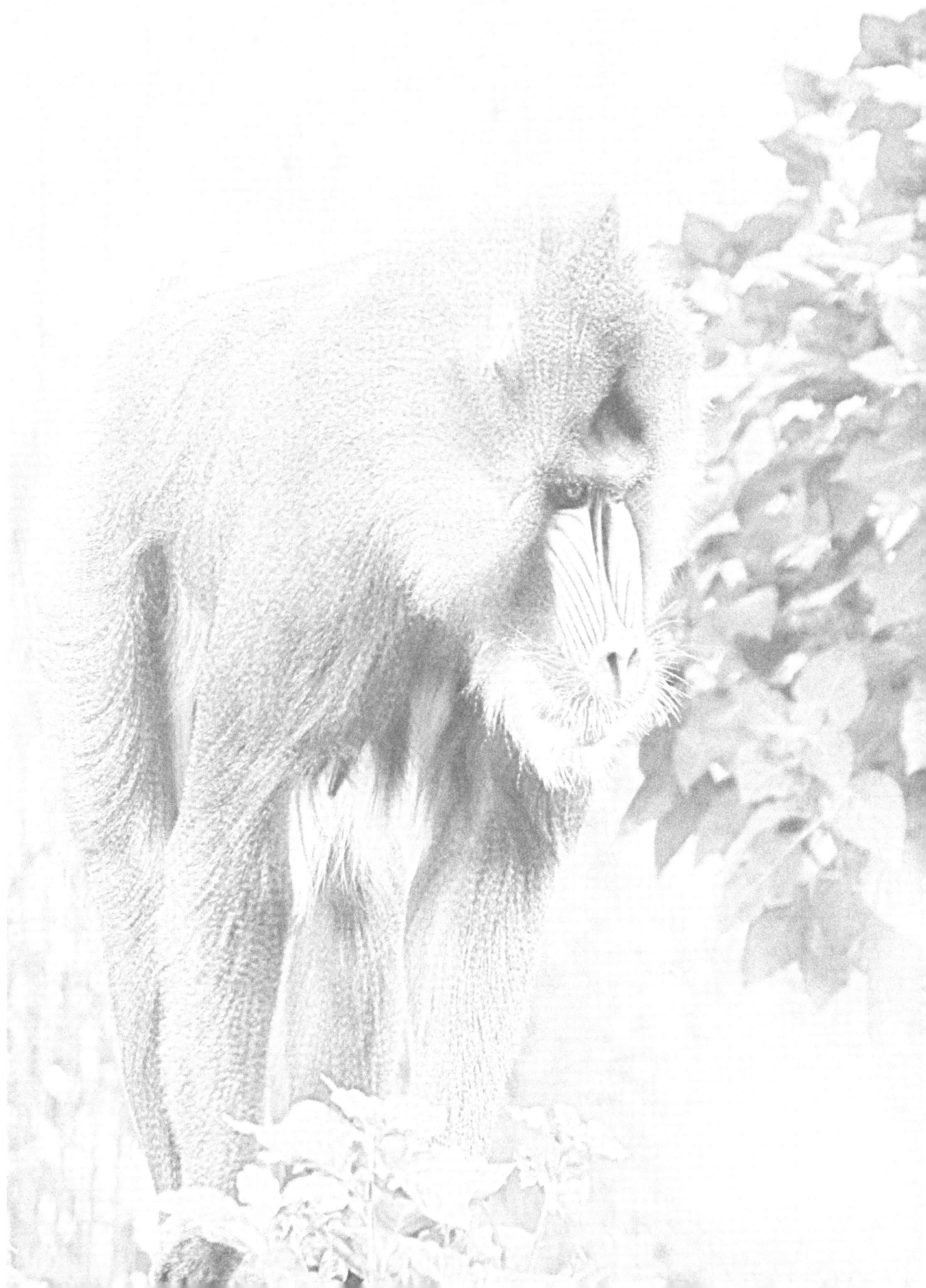

# Merino Sheep

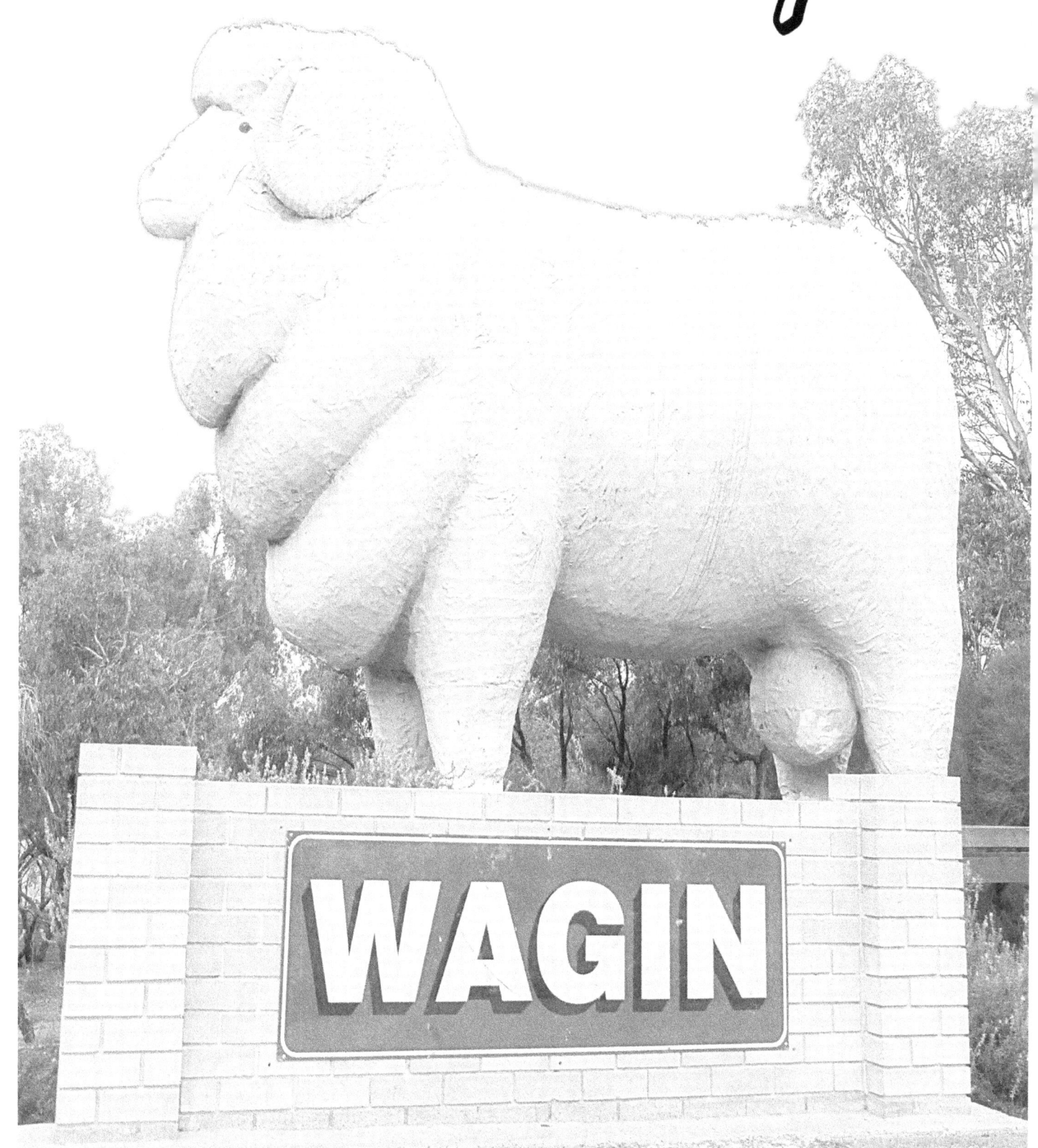

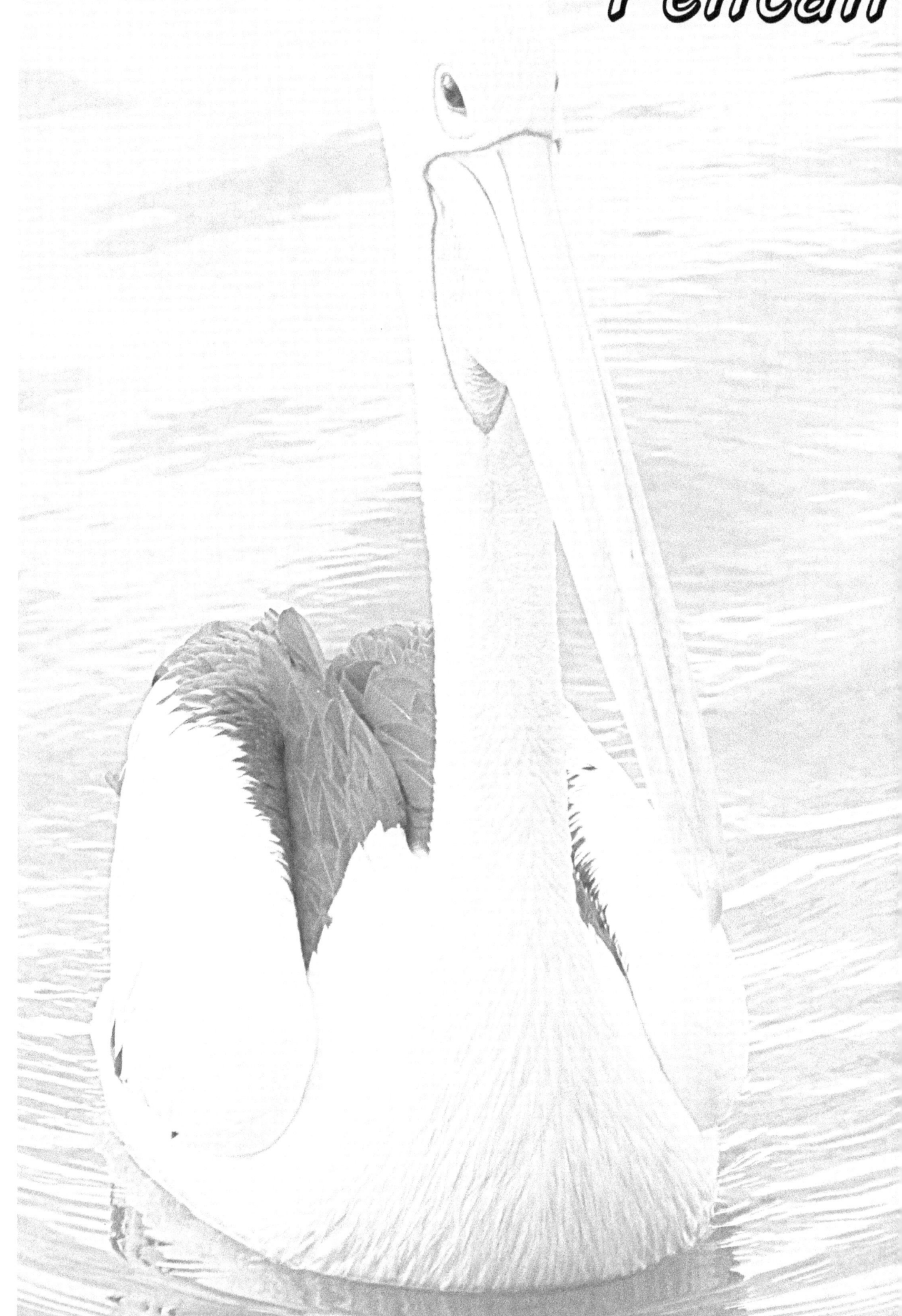

Pelican

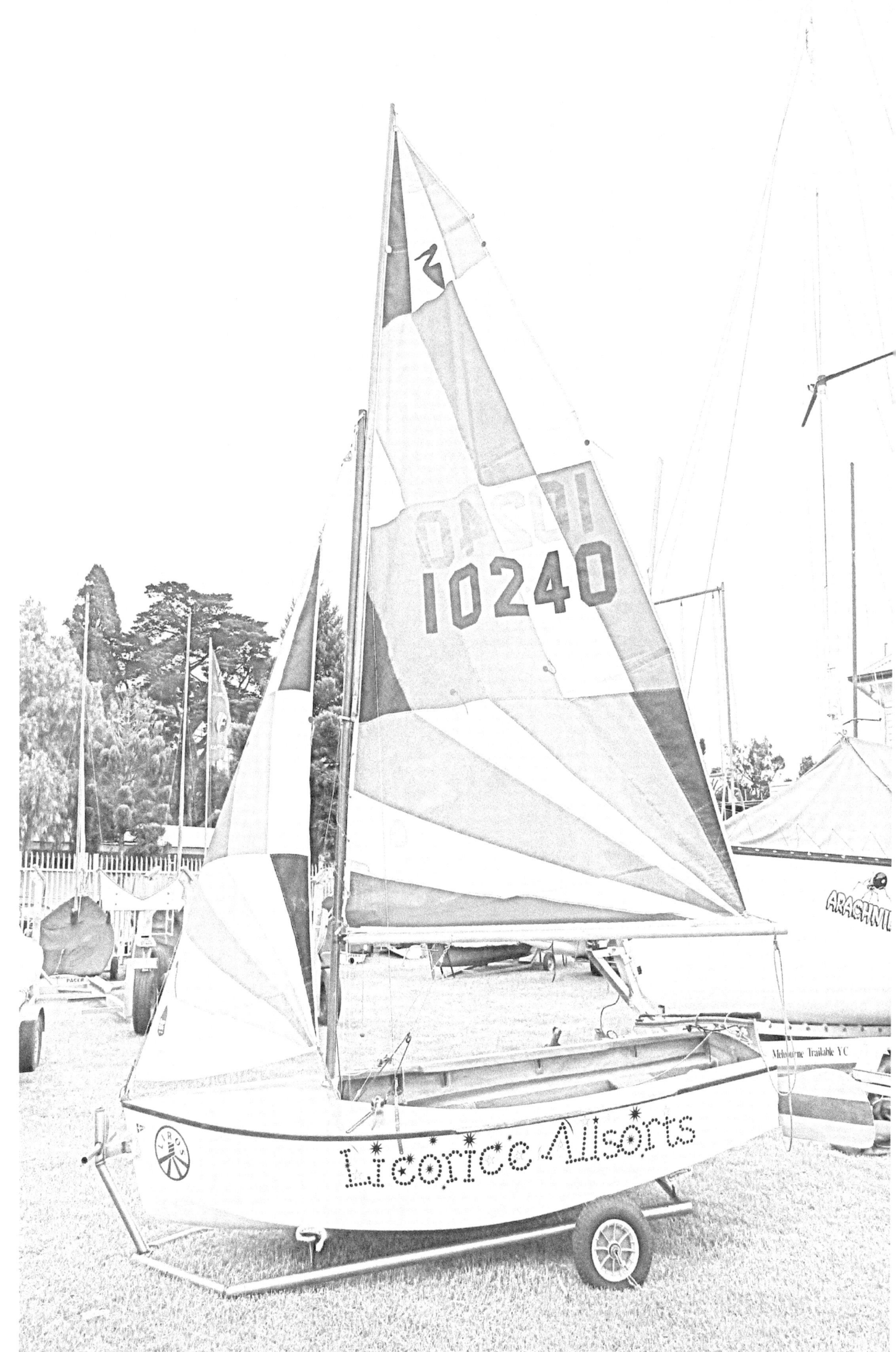